REVISED AND

Understand Your
 DREAMS

Alice Anne Parker

H J KRAMER

NEW WORLD LIBRARY
NOVATO, CALIFORNIA

An H J Kramer Book
published in a joint venture with
New World Library

Editorial office:
H J Kramer Inc
P. O. Box 1082
Tiburon, California 94920

Administrative office:
New World Library
14 Pamaron Way
Novato, California 94949

Editing: Katharine Farnam Conolly
Cover Art: *Seventh Wave* by Hal Kramer
Cover Design: Mary Ann Casler
Cover Photograph: Bosco D'Bruzzi
Typesetting: Tona Pearce Myers

Library of Congress Cataloging-in-Publication Data
Parker, Alice Anne, 1939–
   Understand your dreams / Alice Anne Parker.—Rev. and expanded.
       p.   cm.
   ISBN 0-915811-95-2 (alk. paper)
   1. Dream interpretation. I. Title.
BF1091.P24   2001
154.6'3—dc21   2001002702

First Printing, September 2001
ISBN 0-915811-95-2
Manufactured in Canada on acid-free paper
Distributed to the trade by Publishers Group West

10 9 8 7 6 5 4 3 2 1

With heartfelt thanks to:

Dr. Thomas Maughan
Jane Roberts
Eya Yellin
Alvan Perry Parker

For true symbols have something illimitable about them.
They are inexhaustible in their suggestive and instructive power. . . .
The meanings have to be constantly reread, understood afresh.
And it is anything but an orderly work — this affair of interpreting
the always unpredicted and astonishing metamorphoses.
No systematist who greatly valued his reputation would willingly
throw himself open to the risk of the adventure.
It must, therefore, remain to the reckless dilettante.
Hence the following book.

— Heinrich Zimmer,
The King and the Corpse,
edited by Joseph Campbell

CONTENTS

☾ Acknowledgments

Several years ago, my friend Bosco d'Bruzzi suggested that I write a book on dream images. Like most serious dream workers, I had a powerful aversion to the idea of a dream dictionary, even though I owned a collection of fascinating versions of nineteenth-century bestsellers, including *What Your Dream Meant* by Martini the Palmist.

Then one day as I was leafing through *Heal Your Body*, Louise Hay's invaluable handbook on the metaphysical sources for physical problems, I realized that a comparable book on dream images would be an effective tool for anyone interested in dreams. My friend Sara Halprin suggested that I offer "associations" for the images rather than "meanings," and the book was on its way.

I particularly want to thank Louise Hay for inspiring the design of this book, and for her visionary, yet matter-of-fact, guidance.

I am also indebted to Gabrielle Lusser Rico and Tony Buzan, who independently developed similar techniques of clustering, or arranging information in a pattern of circles, as I have done with dreams.

Rico developed this process of nonlinear brainstorming as a means of stimulating creativity and coherence in student writers in the United States. At the same time, in England, Tony Buzan used a process he called "mapping" as a way of accessing both sides of the brain while organizing a mass of information. I have long used Tony's mapping technique, as described in his book *Use Both Sides of Your Brain*, to play with ideas and organize workshop material, but it wasn't until I read Rico's *Writing the Natural Way* that I saw how useful the clustering process could be for recording dreams.

Each of us is honored by constant friends who support and encourage us through the disappointments that lead to our success. I am privileged to include in this category Tam Mossman, whose expert advice has contributed enormously to my confidence and growth as a writer. My dear friend LaUna Huffines gracefully led me to the perfect publishers, Hal and Linda Kramer. My daughter, April Severson, my husband, Henry Holthaus, and my allies, Freude Bartlett and Mary Kathryn Cope, receive my heartfelt thanks for their years of relentless confidence in my work. This book owes a vast, if unspecifiable, debt to the friendship of Mel Lee, Lana Sawyer, Owen Sawyer, Barbara Such, Peter Bloch, Mary Platt, Kathy Vinton, Herb Long, Harold Cope, Terence Stamp, Sheila Rainer, Pamela Norris, Peggy Donavan, and Herb Goodman. I am also grateful to the members of my Honolulu workshop in Interactive Dreaming, who gave me such useful feedback while I was developing the image catalogue. Thanks to Sandra Brockman, Mary Kathryn Cope, Nancy Crane, Bosco d'Bruzzi, Carla Hayashi, Henry Holthaus, Jan Kaeo, Luana Kuhns, Patricia Martin, Garrett Miyake, Karen Miyake, Georgia Putnam, Jessica Putnam, Doris Rarick, Helen Schlapak, John Squires, and Margaret Stallings.

My thanks also go to all of those who have so generously shared their dreams in my workshops, on *DreamLine*, my radio show, and in the *DreamLine* newspaper column.

I must thank so many "great dreamers" I have worked with during the last five years since the second edition was published, or who have sent me dreams as research material, as their dreams have provided such rich images and stimulating themes. In particular thanks to my daughter, April Severson, a true genius of dreams since babyhood, to Linda Lum, Robin Farris, Sally Klemm, Katy Brook, Bosco d'Bruzzi, Glenn Murray, Athena Lou, Jack Barnett, Sheila Rainer, Xaxa Mason, Darnelle Ovitt, Lori Aquino, Peter Bloch, Sara Halprin, Cassandra Phillips, Carolyn Wolfe, Sarah Small, David Dalton, Lana Sawyer, Margaret Stallings, Marty Garner, Jon Christie, Desiree Madrid, Alba Martinez, and Roy Tjioe.

I owe special thanks to Mayla Blakely for her editing and comments on the new dream images, to Monique Muhlenkamp and Katie Farnam Conolly at New World Library for their attentive support; to my husband, Henry Holthaus, for his unstinting love and encouragement; and, once again, to Linda and Hal Kramer, the kind of publishers authors dream of.

☾ Introduction to the Third Edition

Several months ago I read a review of *Understand Your Dreams* on one of the online bookstores. The woman writing the review praised my book, but said she found the Eight-Step Method too cumbersome to use all the time and wished there was an easier, faster way to get to the meaning of a dream. I agreed. I regularly use a much shorter version in my daily practice and when I teach dream workshops. It's a great tool when I'm working with dreams as a guest on radio shows — where a dream has to be quickly unfolded before listeners tune out. You'll find this shorter Three-Step Method in Part One. And a special thanks to the online reviewer for inspiring me to include the shorter method in this new edition.

Another new feature to make it easier and faster to understand a dream is the comprehensive index at the back of the book, which includes not only each item in the list of Basic Dream Images, but also many synonyms for existing entries. For example, if you dream of a cavern and don't find the image *Cavern* in the Dream Image section, you can look in the index, where you will find this entry: "cavern — see big and cave." Even when you don't find an entry for the image you're seeking, you may find you can combine images on your own. For example, I decided not to include the names of individual trees like maple, oak, and pine. But if you were to have a dream with one of these specific trees in it, you could look up *Tree,* and then the quality you think of when you imagine that particular tree, perhaps *Sugar* for maple, *Mighty* for oak, *Scent* or *Perfume* for pine.

I have also included a large number of descriptive terms in this edition, words like *Alarmed, Afraid, Calm, Deceptive, Dingy,* and *Sleek.* Further, there is an expanded list of action words, like *Buying, Fleeing, Looking, Shielding,* and *Watching,* which often provide a key to identifying the all-important dream territory — Step 1 of the new Three-Step Method.

Your dreams have the potential to activate much greater self-awareness, to offer profound spiritual knowledge, and to give practical guidance for everyday life. I hope this new edition of *Understand Your Dreams* will both illuminate your dream life and lead you to greater fulfillment in your waking life.

May your fondest dreams become glorious waking reality.

— Alice Anne Parker, Hau`ula, Hawaii
April 2001

PART ONE

Remembering and Understanding Your ☾ DREAMS

☾ Dream Work

Over the past thirty-eight years, I've worked with thousands of dreams — my own as well as other people's. And after talking with scores of clients, I've concluded that there are three basic barriers to satisfying dream work.

The first barrier is obvious and all too familiar: *not being able to remember dreams in the first place.* If this is a problem for you, begin by writing down any dream — or dream fragment — that you remember, from any time in your life. Follow the basic steps for processing dreams that I will outline in the next few pages. The simple act of paying close attention to a dream, even one from your distant past, is often enough to stimulate a new pattern of increasing dream recall.

But what if you can't *ever* remember any dream? There is still hope! Instead of recording a dream, record one of your early memories as if it were a dream. Start by recalling a childhood memory — if possible, choose one that resonates with strong emotions — but even a dimly remembered early event will do. Just one or two images, plus the feelings associated with them, will give you plenty to work with. Then, by processing this memory using the basic techniques that follow, you can open a door to the fascinating (and sometimes very practical) messages waiting just across the threshold of your waking consciousness. In most cases, once you have given careful attention to a dream or dreamlike memory, you'll find yourself recalling dreams on a more regular basis.

Now for the second and most common barrier to dream work: *not being able to understand the dreams you do remember.* In this section, I'll be providing you with some basic tools for unfolding the many levels of meaning that most dreams offer you. The index in the second part of this book will give you a head start on making sense of even the most impenetrable dream symbols.

The third barrier to dream work may be the most serious of all: *most of us simply don't have enough time to record our dreams.* No matter how dedicated you are, the pressure of getting kids off to school, the interruption of morning phone calls, and all the demands of your daily rush are there to interfere. With even a few minutes of delay, vital details of a dream can simply evaporate. One of my clients complained of leaving her dream notebook on a corner dresser instead of conveniently close to her bed. By the time she crossed the room, it was too late — the entire dream had faded from her memory.

How can you hope to make sense of what you can no longer remember? Even if you catch your dreams and remember them well, you still need some effective — and *fast* — way of getting them down before they slip away. The following Three-Step and Eight-Step Methods will help you both remember *and* understand your dreams.

☾ The New Three-Step Method

As I mentioned in the introduction, I recently read a review of *Understand Your Dreams* on an online bookstore's website. The reviewer loved the book, but wanted a faster, easier way to get to the meaning of a dream. She found the Eight-Step Method to be thorough, but too time consuming for everyday use. I had to agree, as I often use a shorter method myself.

I'm very pleased to include it here. I believe this new, quick, and easy method will become a tool you use on a daily basis. Most dreams, even big important ones, can be unfolded by asking and answering three questions. What's more — *you don't need to write your dreams down.* Just ask yourself the three questions and most dreams will open up for you.

For years I've been telling people to write down their dreams. I've changed my mind. To use the Three-Step Method you don't need to record your dream. Of course, this is not a new rule to be slavishly followed. You will probably *want* to record memorable dreams. However, you may find you can uncork dream meaning while you're still lying in bed, or over your morning coffee, or even while you're driving to work — without ever writing a single word.

My husband and I share dreams while we're moving through our morning chores — making breakfast, feeding our dogs, Pearl and Ruby, and our aged Siamese cat, Patty Hearst, or while gathering the daily egg from Mrs. Fluffy, our pet chicken. One of us recounts a dream, while the other listens and asks questions. But even if you don't have a handy partner to give you feedback, you can run through the questions on your own, usually in a few short minutes. Here they are:

Step 1: What is the theme of my dream?
Step 2: How do I feel in my dream?
Step 3: When do I have these feelings in my waking life?

It's that simple. However, it's the crucial first step that makes all the difference.

I'll use a few short dreams as examples of how to use the new Three-Step Method, starting with a weird and wonderful food dream recently sent to me by a contributor.

I'm driving my car, leaning out of the window and scraping up blacktop, which I am eating. It's delicious and crunchy, like the crust on savory brownies. I have a feeling that it's not good for me to eat so much of it, but it's so tasty, I can't stop. When I look in the mirror my eyes are red from eating the blacktop and I'm worried about being able to see the road.

Step 1:
What Is the Theme of My Dream?

What exactly *is* the theme of a dream? You could think of it as the realm of the dream or the field of the dream, the internal theme or premise that underlies the action — what the dream is really trying to tell you underneath all the action and details. For example, "the falling dream" — one of the most common fear dreams, shared by humans everywhere, during every period of history — is probably not warning you to stay away from high places. Instead, it appears at a time of opportunity, a time when something you've hoped for and prepared for is about to happen, and you're just not sure you'll make it. The key action word, *falling,* and the feelings associated with it, will point you towards the central theme, a fear of *loss of control.*

In order to discover the theme of a dream you might ask the question, "What is this dream about?" But it's actually more than that. A better question would be "What is this dream *really* all about?" The dream theme is not the events, nor the characters, nor even the relationships. It's the internal core, the essence, the story behind the story you tell when you recount your dream.

To identify the dream theme or territory, it usually works best to start with the action or the action words and look them up in the Basic Dream Images. This dreamer is driving his car. Driving and cars in dreams almost always represent power, our ability to get where we're going. But the dreamer is also eating, so the dream territory has something to do with how he nourishes himself. Put these two together and you might identify the dream theme like this: *This dream is about something I'm doing to nourish myself that I'm afraid isn't too good for me and which may affect my ability to reach my destination.*

Another simpler way to state the theme of this dream, would be to say — *This dream is about my power and how I nurture myself.*

For some of us a very few words will be enough; others will prefer a more complex, detailed statement about the dream theme.

Step 2:
How Do I Feel in My Dream?

This dreamer might say he was really *enjoying himself* at first, then had the feeling that *what he was doing wasn't good for him,* but *he still couldn't stop,* even though *he was worried* about not being able to see the road. In the dream he has a sequence of feelings, and it is important to identify each feeling in turn.

Step 3:
When Do I Have This Feeling in My Waking Life?

To answer this question, you must step away from the activity in your dream for a moment and think about your daily life. While imagining how you felt in your dream, think about when you have these same feelings in your everyday activities or at certain times during your life. Remember to identify these feelings in the same order you felt them in your dream. You should be able to quickly identify several possibilities or maybe hone in on one distinct time that you feel or have felt this way.

The question to ask our dreamer would be "When in your waking life do you feel there is something you enjoy that isn't good for you, but that you just can't stop, even though you're worried it will prevent you from reaching your goal?"

Here we will have to speculate. In his waking life this dreamer could actually be eating something that he feels is not good for him, but that he loves and continues to indulge in, even though he fears it is detrimental to his health in some way.

Looking up two crucial images from the dream, *Mirror* and *Eyes,* could lead to another possibility. *Mirror* is associated with *Identity*, and with the question, *What am I ready to see? Eyes* are associated with *Vision, Consciousness, Clarity.* The questions to ask when eyes are important in a dream are *What am I aware of?* and *How do I see the world?* These images might suggest that some appetite he over-indulges, which affects his consciousness and clarity, may prevent him from achieving a goal of greater awareness.

Only the dreamer will know if the three questions have been accurately and adequately answered.

How will you, as dreamer, know when it's right? You'll feel it. You'll have an *aha* experience — when the dream opens up for you, offering its insights and advice.

Let's go through the steps with a few more short dreams. Here's another with a common theme:

My husband and I have almost reached the top of the stairs. Suddenly, the dark woman races up behind us and stabs me in the back.

Stairs, elevators, mountains — we seem to spend a lot of time going up and down in dreams. If we're going up, the dream is usually talking about larger awareness, greater consciousness, achievement; going down, we're moving into the territory of the unconscious self, exploring the roots of issues or attitudes.

What does it mean when you say someone has stabbed you in the back? You've been betrayed.

This dream theme might be described thusly: *This dream is about my feeling that just when I've almost reached what I most aspire to, I'm suddenly betrayed.*

When I asked this contributor what she felt in the dream, she replied that at first she was filled with a "marvelous sense of fulfillment"

— the height of her ambition was about to be realized. Then, she added, just as she took the last step, she was "stopped cold by betrayal."

I asked if these feelings were present in her waking life and who the dark woman might be? She replied that she believed herself to be at the very threshold of creative recognition, which filled her with wonderful exhilaration. She believed the dark woman represented her fear that, once again, she would be disappointed. She added that she believed this inner self might sabotage her and prevent her from realizing her potential.

I suggested that she might take this dream a step further by considering the associations for *Dark* in the list of Basic Dream Images. These associations — *Mystery, The unknown and unformed,* and *A place of fear or of potential* — suggest another possibility. By asking herself the questions listed with *Dark* — *For what do I search?* and *What seeks to take form?* — she may discover an unexpected ally in the dark woman. A bad dream calls attention forcefully and irresistibly to the area that is ready for healing. By acknowledging and processing the fear the dark woman represents, this dreamer can open the way to the recognition she's hoping for.

Here's a more complicated, but fascinating dream in which the image of fear becomes a means of salvation:

I'm naked, floating in a sea of darkness, when something brushes my stomach and I intuitively know a shark is circling. I panic until the shark starts talking to me in an erudite manner, saying, "I can see you are in a bit of a predicament and I would like to offer you my services as a sleeping bag." I realize just how cold I am. The shark lowers itself vertically, opens wide, and holds me inside without so much as a nibble. I feel grateful for the gentle protection of this powerful ocean predator.

Another common pattern — dreams of swimming, floating, ocean, sea — water in all its myriad forms, usually speak to us about our feelings. The bigger the body of water, the more profound the feelings involved. And what about that friendly shark? A talking animal is a big deal in a dream. Here information is coming from the primal depths, the deepest levels of magical communication and natural wisdom. Let's look at this dream more closely, following the three steps.

What is the theme of her dream?

Here's where the list of Basic Dream Images will be a big help. If you look up *Naked,* you'll find the associations *Exposed* and *Vulnerable* and the question *Where am I ready to be seen?* The image, *Ocean* (the synonym for *Sea*), gives additional information as associations: *Vast, limitless feeling. Sometimes an overwhelming emotion.* Checking *Shark* would give you a further question, *What powerful feeling is threatening me?*

You might translate the dream theme like this: *When it comes to deep feelings, I'm exposed and cold until I receive protection from the very dangers that I fear.*

You will notice that the one line describing the dream theme is very condensed. When a dream is as powerful as this one, you'll probably want to go much further with it. For example, identifying exactly what kind of threat or danger the shark represents, considering just what it means that the danger in the dream is transformed *after* it is understood as potential protection, and that *getting inside* the threat is crucial to the change.

Another, somewhat simpler way of stating the dream theme could be this: *Exposure to deep feelings has chilled and frightened me; now I'm ready to get inside my fears.*

How does she feel in this dream?

She begins by feeling *vulnerable* and *cold*. She *panics,* but after accepting the shark's offer of help, she is *grateful* for its protection.

When is this feeling present in her waking life?

She might ask herself when in her waking life has trust transformed a potential threat into a means of protection.

Another short dream with a very common theme:

I was in this amazing house with many stories. I noticed beautiful furnishings that became more interesting as we climbed each floor. I had been to all of the floors except the top floor, the fourth. On the fourth floor there were spirits and I was scared. My counselor was there with me, but I left soon after that. She wasn't bothered at all.

Houses. We dream of moving in and moving out of our childhood homes, of houses and apartments we have lived in or never actually lived in, but which are as familiar to us as if we had lived there for years. Welcome to one of the great, most common dream subjects — the house of the self.

In this delicious dream, it's an *amazing* house of *many* stories. And it gets even better as the dreamer climbs higher to a larger awareness of who she is and how beautiful and interesting she is. Only when she reaches the portentous fourth floor does she get scared. Now this is a bit tricky. I looked up the number *Four* in Basic Dream Images and found these associations: *Stability. Matter. Strength. Worldly effort.* In someone else's dreams these might be crucial associations, but I know this person and I know she does a regular self-healing meditation that uses the chakra system. *What is the fourth chakra? The chakra of the heart.*

How is this as a statement of the dream theme? *As I explore my true self, I'm amazed at my own beauty, at how interesting I am — until I reach the level of my heart, where I'm afraid.*

It's impossible for me to leave this dream without commenting on the role of the counselor. This is a real person representing herself, of course, but she is also a projection of the dreamer's higher self, the part of her who knows and is comfortable at the level of the heart, where the spirits abide.

How does this dreamer feel?

At first she is *amazed* and *interested*. She becomes *scared*, but embodied in her counselor, we can see the potential for her to neutralize her fear — her fear is ready to be changed to a *lack of concern*.

When is this feeling present in her waking life?

We might assume that this dreamer is finding the process of personal growth to be a source of fascination and interest. With the help of good counsel, she is preparing to address her fears in order to fully occupy the house of the larger self.

Let's try another short dream with extraordinary images:

I'm trying to tell someone something, but I have bubble gum in my mouth. It has a strange, gooey texture, like it starts to fall apart if you try to take it out of your mouth. I'm pulling and pulling, but I can't get it all out. It seems to be multiplying and feels like it's going down my throat. It is so frustrating and kind of scary.

I am so delighted when I hear a completely new dream, especially one with such vivid, alarming images. Although I'll have to admit that when I received this dream from a correspondent only a week ago, I had to quickly add *Gum* to the expanded list of Basic Dream Images in this new edition so I could include the dream here. What's more, I'm a bit stumped by it. The dreamer wrote that she thought the dream might be about her fear of expressing herself in confrontational situations. She actually knows someone who had exactly the same dream and they discovered they shared this reluctance, even though they're both great communicators in general.

What is the theme of this dream?

Let's see what happens when we look for the dream theme. *Can't speak* is a common dream experience, one that has been reported to me over and over again, although it's usually a case of not being able to make a sound — there's no gum involved. Let's see what happens when we put the two together. Associations for *can't speak* are *Retreat* and *Loss of identity*, with the question, *What will happen if I make myself heard?* For *Gum*, the association is *Release of nervous tension*, the question, *What relaxes me?*

Let's restate the dream using some of the above material: *When I'm in confrontation situations I feel like I've got a big wad of bubble gum in my mouth that I can't get out.* Now we'll add one more piece of information. What kind of gum is it? Bubble gum. Who chews bubble gum? Kids. Now we have an important connection. Let's see if it works for dream theme: *When I'm in confrontational situations I feel like a kid, not an adult who can make herself heard.*

How did this dreamer feel in the dream?

All we know is that she wakes with feelings of *frustration* and *fear*. As in the dream of the dark woman on the staircase, I think this dream may offer a potential solution to the perceived problem with confrontation. What does gum do? It releases nervous tension and relaxes the chewer.

When is this feeling present in her waking life?

We already know that the contributor feels this way in confrontational situations. She may want to play with the idea of confrontation being like a contest between kids to see who can blow the biggest bubble. Sometimes something as simple as reframing a situation in the terms of the dream can lead to a disarmingly indirect solution to an old problem. Behind this dream may be a suggestion that a spirit of lighthearted play will ease the old tensions associated with confrontational situations.

Let's look at one more dream, going through all three questions:

I dream I had made a decision not to can food. I was stand-ing in the middle of our kitchen with those tall, white cup-boards, COMPLETELY empty. I knew it was my fault for not restocking them, but I just didn't want to do it. I turned away and facing me was a school of salmon, ready to spawn. They hadn't eaten for months, their bodies had changed to hooked mouths and humps on their backs; and they began to change color. These salmon were literally dying in front of me and I had nothing to feed them (no canned beans, toma-toes, and beets, which we all know salmon adore). I knew these salmon as my family and close friends. I was completely distressed and so agitated that I woke up bawling.

Like the earlier shark dream, this is a big dream, profound and powerful. If it were mine I would probably record it meticulously and use every step of the Eight-Step Method to extract each bit of meaning and value from it. However, let's see how far we can go with it, using only the new Three-Step Method.

What is the theme of this dream?

It's every serious housekeeper's nightmare. Just when you realize the cupboards are completely bare, a whole load of company arrives unexpectedly and they're starving. The cupboards are empty because the dreamer hasn't taken care of her business of *preserving,* thus the salmon won't be able to fulfill their destiny to spawn before they die, which somehow makes them like the dreamer's family and friends. Let's restate that as a single sentence. *Failure to nurture leads to a fail-ure to procreate, and therefore family and friends do without.*

It helps that I know this dreamer is a woman in her late thirties, recently divorced, who did not have children with her first husband, and who is not yet ready to commit to a new permanent relationship.

But even if I didn't know these things, bare cupboards and spawning salmon would direct me towards this theme. Let's extend the sentence above to see if it can cover the dream theme: *Failure to preserve leads to failure to nurture, which leads to failure to procreate, and family and friends do without.*

Not exactly an elegant sentence, but it does seem to do the trick. On to Step 2.

How does she feel in the dream?

What is that first feeling — when she's looking in the bare cupboards, but knows she just didn't want to do it? It might be *guilt,* but there's also a *sense of resolution.* She really *didn't want to do it.* Next she feels *distressed* and *so agitated* that she wakes *crying.*

Now to Step 3.

Where is this feeling present in her waking life?

I would guess that she feels a bit guilty about not having had children yet, but doesn't regret not having had them with her ex. Nevertheless she's distressed and agitated. Like those poor hungry salmon, she may not bear children at all. And, of course, she feels everyone suffers, since family, most friends, and our very culture still expects us to procreate — and damn it, she wants to!

Anytime a dream ends in terror or tears, there's a further step that I strongly recommend you take. It's the seventh step in the Eight-Step Method:

What changes would you like to make in this dream?

Remember, the dream isn't telling you how it is, it's telling you how you *feel* it is at this moment in time. And if you feel terror or have tears at the end of the dream, it is of the utmost importance that you create a new final act, a new ending to the dream.

The options are endless. The dreamer above could open the fridge to discover *lots* of tasty salmon food, which might also suggest that her own eggs have been safely chilled and are just waiting for the right partner to come along and warm them up. It's not too late after all. The salmon can survive, and she can fulfill her own destiny, as well.

Please go to page 30 to learn how to work with the new ending in your own dream, once you have found one that satisfies you.

Please remember, the key to dream understanding is always feeling.

How do you feel when you identify the dream theme or answer the other questions? You'll know it's right when it *feels* right to you.

How did you feel in the dream itself? This is the clearest message the dream gives you about the events of your waking life. How do you feel about a particular object in the dream, or a person, or activity? To one dreamer a banquet might be a boring ritual; to another, it could mean long sought-after acknowledgment. *Formal celebration* and *Recognition,* the associations listed in Basic Dream Images, would have different significance for each dreamer. Yet, once the feeling has been identified, the appropriate meaning and connection can unfold.

What to Do When You Can't Quickly Identify the Dream Theme

By now you may also be wondering how well this method will work for you if you don't automatically connect *nakedness* with vulnerability, *sea* with emotions, or think of *sharks* as the dangers lurking in emotions as we did with our shark dream. If you don't get these connections right away, don't be frustrated. Looking up these images gives you solid information on a likely theme or territory of the dream.

Of course this means you may need to glance at the images in the book while you're making breakfast or feeding your pet chicken, although preferably not while you're driving to work. Nailing the dream theme may take a bit more time and work at first. However, you will quickly get the knack of identifying dream themes, especially the familiar themes that recur in your dreams on a regular basis. The more practice you have, the more clearly the answers to the questions will appear.

Identifying emotions can help you find the dream theme.

If you find yourself completely confused about the theme of a dream, go on to Steps 2 and 3, *How did I feel in the dream?* and *When is this feeling present in my waking life?* Then go back to Step 1, *What is the theme of my dream?* For some, listing the emotions of the dream and connecting them to waking life circumstances makes it much easier to identify the dream theme.

It's also important to feel if the associations and questions to be asked in the list of Basic Dream Images are right for you.

Like many of you, I've had the experience of looking up a dream image, checking the associations or questions and thinking, "No, that's not it at all." Usually this happens when the image means something specific to me or to the particular dream. However, even when the personal meaning of the image is far removed from what is in the book, reading these associations often triggers the correct interpretation for me — seeing what it *isn't* leads me to what it *is*.

When feelings are clear in a dream, it is relatively easy to quickly identify or list them.

Often, however, feelings are ambiguous, particularly when you are a neutral observer in a dream, not present as a character, just watching the action. That, in fact, is the information you will work with. How did you feel in the dream? *Like a neutral observer, not present, just watching.* In Step 3 you will ask yourself, when do you have this same feeling (or absence of feeling) in your waking life — a particularly important question when the dream involves a situation or action where it would be usual for someone to feel strong emotions.

If you are often a neutral observer in dreams you might identify the feeling you would like to have or that you feel would be usual, given the action of the dream. Then, for Step 3, you might look to see if this same feeling is also frequently absent in your waking life.

The healing power of dreams.

Dreams do their healing work for you every night while you sleep. They are healing you whether you remember them or not, whether you write them down or not, whether you understand them, or ignore them. What a friend we have in dreams!

Be easy on yourself.

Dream work doesn't need to be *work*. If you fail to interpret a dream or to write it down, it will still recur, in one form or another. There is a part of you that knows what you have come to do and who you have come to be. It will continue to give you nightly bulletins, some profoundly supportive and reassuring, some deeply arousing or challenging — until you get the message.

Treat your dreams with respect and attention and welcome all they have to offer you. It is my heartfelt wish that by welcoming these nightly messengers you will experience the answers you seek. Dreams are natural. Good or bad dreams, troubling or inspiring dreams, all exist with the same purpose — to bring each of us to a place of greater inner peace, of good health and harmony. By tuning ourselves with these exquisitely conceived nightly performances, we can find the deep harmony that exists inside us all.

May your fondest dreams come true!

☾ An Eight-Step Method

Step 1:
Record the Images of Your Dream.

Dreams often have a funny way of happening all at once. They don't occur in a linear, one-two-three sequence, as do events in waking life. Writing them down in narrative paragraphs not only takes too long, but it often violates the sense of the original dream in which events relate and interconnect in a much more circular, holistic, and organic form. So rather than write your dream down, try dropping dream images into an easy-to-draw pattern of circles.

This takes much less time than the usual way of writing out a dream one sentence at a time, and also allows you to relate dream events to each other in a more flowing and flexible form. Just drop the dream's main images into a pattern of circles and then let the information cook while you get on with your day. For each element, draw a circle large enough to express the importance of each image or event. Use one big circle to "enclose" a few words that describe the central action, perhaps with smaller surrounding circles to represent the sequence of events. Don't feel it's necessary to duplicate the perfect circles of the following patterns. Quickly sketch a rough circle and jot down the basic images. See below for some examples of possible patterns.

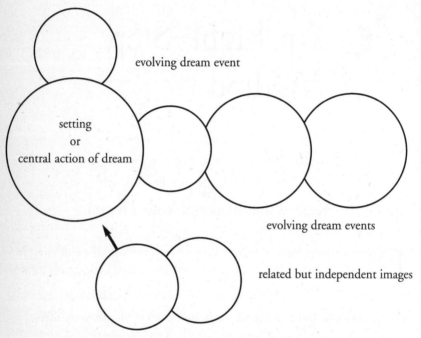

evolving dream event

setting
or
central action of dream

evolving dream events

related but independent images

You may wish to connect the circles with arrows or symbols.

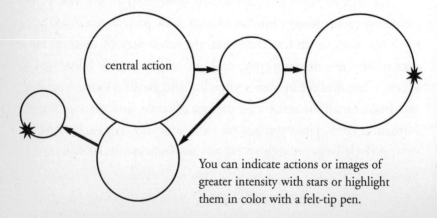

central action

You can indicate actions or images of greater intensity with stars or highlight them in color with a felt-tip pen.

With this technique, you can quickly record all of the dream's main components — more than enough to jog your memory later, when you have time to review the diagram. This method is not only faster than writing out a dream in complete sentences, but also gives you a more accurate record of the original experience. The "splash pattern" diagram allows you to relate dream events to one another in a more flowing and flexible form.

It may take a few mornings for you to become completely comfortable with this new system, but it will allow you to record even long and complex dreams quickly, even when you are particularly rushed.

Step 2:
What Word or Phrase Best Expresses Your Feeling in This Dream?

You can tackle Step 2 as you are driving to work or sitting quietly with a second cup of coffee in the morning, or in the evening before you go to bed. Ask yourself, "How did I feel in my dream?" or "How did the dream make me feel?"

The answer should be easy, if sometimes a bit ambiguous: "curious," "worried," and "confused" are common replies. With a bad dream, the answer may be "anxious," or even "terrified." An ecstatic dream may produce a "blissful" feeling; my own very favorite dreams leave me with a feeling that everything is just fine, that things are all coming together perfectly.

Often, though, the answer you give yourself will be a bit more complex, as in "I wonder why I haven't lived in all these beautiful rooms!" Or "I can't figure out how to get my bags packed in time and I'm afraid I'll miss the flight!" Here, your clues lie in the emotionally evocative words: *I wonder why I haven't lived...*," "*I can't figure out...*," and "*I'm afraid I'll miss....*"

Step 3:
When Is This Same Feeling Present in Your Waking Life?

Tracking down the source of each feeling can be a bit tricky, but in most cases you will feel an immediate tingle of recognition, and some particular area or issue in your life will leap into focus. Using the examples given under Step 2, you might discover that you haven't lived out your childhood dreams, that you can't figure out how to pack all the "baggage" of accumulated attitudes and beliefs and still "make the flight" to a greater awareness of what's really going on in your life.

By asking and answering these questions, you begin to use the valuable insights that every night's dreams offer you with such inventive guidance.

Step 4:
What Were the Significant Activities in Your Dream?

List the key activities in your dream, and turn to Part Two. For each action, look up the associations given in the second column and the questions in the third column. If the associations and questions seem appropriate, write your answers down, especially if you've been dreaming about the same activities over a considerable period of time.

At first, some of these "typical" dream activities may be hard for you to pinpoint. Many of us have regular dream patterns that have become so familiar that we may take them completely for granted. For example, do you always find yourself hunting for a new apartment, fighting the enemy, going shopping, finding bills and coins, or trying to get a decent meal? I have been traveling in my dreams for my entire life. This activity seemed so natural and ordinary that I never examined the meaning behind it. Instead, I usually focused my attention on the method of traveling and the inevitable delays and problems en route, completely failing to notice that the essential framework of my dreams was so often a journey. It was a real breakthrough when I finally noticed that these dreams were giving me pithy bulletins on my personal *bildungsroman,* my inner search for the best routes and the most direct passage to my goal of greater consciousness. I continue to be on the road in many of my dreams, but now I'm more alert to the deeper meaning of these regular travel updates!

So consider the activities of your dream, particularly if they are familiar to you from many previous recurrent dreams. Look up these activities in Part Two of this book and see if the associations given seem appropriate to you. Sometimes these associations may not fit for you, but often just seeing what *isn't* perfectly accurate will stimulate you to come up with a more exact answer. Then ask yourself the question or questions that appear in the right-hand column. Again, even if these questions don't quite fit, they will usually give you a clue to the question you *do* need to ask.

Working with a Partner

Active dreaming is a lot more fun if you have someone you can use as a sounding board. Sometimes simply having someone else ask you the questions in the right-hand column of Part Two will help stimulate an answer. Sharing a dream dialogue with your partner or mate, with other family members, or with a good friend enriches everyone's dreams and the collective awareness as well. Remember that increased consciousness is highly contagious.

Step 5:
List the Characters in Your Dream.

What Part of You Does Each Dream Figure Represent?

For Step 5, list the "cast" of your dream — the figures and characters who appeared in it — and examine them one by one. If they are real people known to you personally, they may represent themselves or your feelings about them: your wife is really your wife, your friend your friend, and so on. In unfolding the dream's meaning, however, you will find it useful to describe these familiar persons with a word or two: "My wife is *capable* and *extravagant*." "My friend is *weak willed* but *well intentioned*."

Now, a slightly tougher assignment: Ask what *aspects* of yourself are reflected by these various dream figures. In other words, in what ways are *you* being capable and extravagant? How are *you* judging yourself as weak willed but well intentioned? Also, look up *Wife* and *Friend* to see what general associations those relationships may present for you.

When apparent strangers play a part in your dream script, you can look up their roles or professions in Part Two. For *Dentist,* for example, the given association is *Work on independence and power.* If these associations feel appropriate to you, then ask the questions listed for each character; for *Dentist,* the question is *What part of me needs strengthening?*

Step 6:
List the Significant Places, Objects, Colors, and Events in the Dream.

Once again, if the associations and questions listed feel relevant to your dream, write down your answer.

If your dream dentist in Step 5 was working on your teeth, you will find for *Teeth* the further associations of *Independence, Power. Ability to nourish and communicate.* Here, the questions to ask yourself are "Where in my life do I fear dependence?" and "What do I wish to say?"

List all the objects, places, colors, and events of your dream — especially ones that seem particularly vivid or noticeably unusual or out of place. In most dreams, certain places and objects will be prominent. When you remember the dream later, they will stand out with greater detail, or else you will sense a stronger emotional field around them. When you look up their associations and the questions to ask yourself, pay particular attention to these stronger images.

The associations given in Part Two are usually neutral or positive. If you dream about an angry dog, for example, you will find *Dog* associated with the positive qualities of loyalty and trustworthiness. If your dream dog seemed threatening to you, adjust the questions accordingly. Ask yourself, "Where do I feel *threatened* by lack of loyalty?" or "What do I *not* trust in myself?"

The list of images presented here cannot be exhaustive, of course. Anything you can imagine (and many things you haven't imagined!) will turn up in dreams. But, to track down the meanings and associations of these images, you can use related objects or ideas as clues. For example, if you dream that your teeth are falling out, you may be distressed to find that there is no listing for that exact image. But looking up both *Teeth* and *Falling* will lead you to the exciting questions *Where in my life do I fear dependence?* and *Where do I want to land?*

Perhaps, for you, fear of dependence has been a hurdle to intimate relationships, making you afraid to fall in love. Yet with this dream's help, you might discover that you really want to "land" in the kind of supportive and trusting relationship you have always longed for.

Personal Dream Vocabularies

Most of us have expanded dream vocabularies based on the interests and specialties of our waking life. In one of my dream workshops, an interior designer regularly reported dreams with richly detailed images featuring elaborate patterns and textures. To understand these dreams, she began by working with the primary associations for images such as *Walls, Carpet, Furniture, Chair, Antiques, Colors,* and so on. To follow the more subtle levels of meaning, however, she had to take the further step of asking herself what she felt about each image's specific details.

One of the interior designer's dreams featured two chairs; the first she described as an original Louis XV side chair upholstered in lovat green silk jacquard. The chair was beautiful and valuable, but also stiff, fragile, and quite uncomfortable; this, she concluded, represented her discomfort with old principles and attitudes. The second chair, a copy from a later historical period, was less valuable, but much more useful.

She then considered each specific detail, seeking more personal levels of meaning. It was an education in style to hear her examine the precise significance of Louis XV versus Directoire, of lovat green versus viridian, of jacquard weave versus petit point. As she pursued each detail of these designs, more and more information unfolded about changes she was preparing to make — both professionally and personally.

When you work with rich imagery derived from your own areas of interest, ask yourself how you feel about the particular details in the dream that have caught your attention. Personal levels of association will quickly expand the general meanings and questions provided in Part Two of this book.

Sample Dream Analysis

Here's an example of steps 1 through 6, taken from my own dream journal. The dream story was brief, but significant. First, let me report the dream in conventional linear form:

> *I am driving in a car with my old friend Joan. We are cutting class together to go swimming. I am feeling very pleased to have this time with her. Then I am leaving my daughter April at the train station. I feel a bit worried about her having all of the details of her journey together and making her connection to the boat on time.*

I am uncertain which part of the dream happened first.

Using the circle technique of Step 1, I could easily and rapidly fit these two events or images into two large circles, thus:

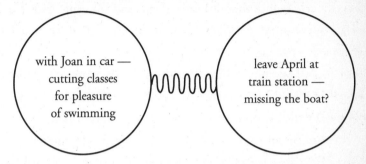

Since I wasn't sure which part of the dream happened first, I drew an odd wiggly line between the two circles. The activities seemed to offer different choices of behavior — as if one balanced, or excluded, the other.

Now for Step 2: What word or phrase best expresses your feeling in this dream? First I wrote the phrase "missing the boat!" That was my strongest feeling. I had awakened with the familiar sense of excitement, coupled with that special anxiety that ship's whistles or train timetables can provoke in me. "Will we make it on time?" Then I also wrote: "*Worried* that I don't stay with April — but *pleased* to spend time with Joan."

Step 3: When is this same feeling present in your waking life? Ouch! No tingle of recognition for me. As soon as I thought about these emotions, the sensation was more like a nasty twinge in the back of my neck. "With regard to work and ambition," I wrote, "I am worried that I will miss the 'boat' of success — yet also, I believe that I already know what I need to know and that I can 'cut classes' to give time to old friends."

I noticed that in my journal I skipped Step 4, the question about identifying significant dream activities — but I'll return to that later. Now, Step 5: What part of you does each dream figure represent? I started by considering the characteristics of my daughter April, who was then a student at a prestigious university. She seemed to represent fulfillment of ambition to me. I also added that she knew how to enjoy herself and that I felt a deep and abiding love for her. Translating this information I saw that she embodied — or reflected — these traits for me.

For Joan, I wrote, "failure of ambition," "pleasure denying," and "betrayal of friendship." That is, I saw her as someone who had not fulfilled her early ambitions, who had denied herself many pleasures, and who had betrayed our friendship. I realized that she represented the part of me that feels like a failure, denies joy, and withholds love. Not a pretty picture!

After you have worked through the relevant associations and questions prompted by your dreams, you will have a good idea of what areas and issues in your life are clamoring for transformation. Now, instead of remaining the passive observer of events, you can become an active participant in your dream creation.

Step 7:
What Changes, If Any, Would You Like to Make in This Dream?

Even a bad dream is a stimulus for change, pointing out where you are ready to grow. Simply because a bad dream *is* so powerful, it forcefully draws your attention to whatever area of your life is ready for work. A nightmare — about teeth falling out, for example — may be pointing the way to a joyous, committed partnership. Just recognizing that fact is a step in the right direction.

And, then, *decide what changes, if any, you would like to make in the dream.* Each and every element of your dream belongs to you. You can change it as you wish, and you will benefit directly and dramatically from the energy you release by doing so. It is almost always easier to make the change in a dream *before* you attempt a similar transformation in your waking life. Once you do so, you can trust that similar changes will begin to appear in your waking life.

Begin by imagining different endings to your dream, particularly if it is part of a pattern or series that has been cropping up again and again for any length of time. Rewriting your dream script is not mere wishful thinking. When you play around with alternative solutions, you are using what is sometimes called "lateral thinking" — creative, playful manipulation of the images generated by the deepest levels of your own consciousness to resolve what are often lifelong issues and limitations.

When you find a really satisfying solution to a longtime dream problem, review your new plan as you are falling to sleep. If, like me, you find yourself constantly traveling around, enduring the hassles of too-tight schedules and missing suitcases, then maybe it's time you chartered your own plane! In your imagination, declare that your flight will leave when *you* are ready, baggage and all, and not before. You'll even have time to go back for the red suitcase that fell out of the back of the car as you were racing to the airport.

Start by rerunning your dream in one of its familiar forms, but then graft the new ending in place. When you go to sleep, expect the dream to reappear with some surprising new twists, but now you are ready to resolve it with new solutions or a creative alternative — and be confident that you will wake up with a great feeling of success.

Going back to the previous example from my dream journal, I resolved to make a conscious change in that rather unsettling dream. What changes would I like to make in this dream? What parts of it did I enjoy? I wrote, "I would like to stay at the train station until April is aboard the train, thus guaranteeing that she will not miss the boat. I enjoyed the other part of the dream, knowing it was okay to take time away from studies to swim and talk with Joan. I felt we could rebuild our lost friendship."

Changing Bad Dreams into Good Ones

Several years ago, I worked with a woman who related a classic recurrent nightmare. In her dream, she would awaken to hear someone entering her house. All the appropriate creaks would sound, and she would hear slow, heavy footsteps coming down the hallway toward her bedroom. Frozen with terror, she would be unable to call to her roommates for help. As the door slowly swung open in the dream, she would awaken for real — to find herself in bed, trembling with fear.

In my client's first breakthrough with this dream, she found herself on a sailboat, watching her recurrent nightmare unfold on the screen of a television set. At first, she identified with the horror movie and was enormously frightened. But then, realizing that it was only a show on TV, she walked up to the set and changed the channel.

The dream had terrorized my client for years, and she dreaded its appearance. It was understandably difficult for her to approach it as an opportunity — to anticipate it and be ready to change it. I was very pleased to see her reverse this pattern: By watching the event take place on a TV screen, she was distancing herself from the fear and was genuinely prepared to "turn the old story off."

After this, however, my client experienced several very frightening dreams that escalated in terror. She also had a lurking fear that the dream was precognitive, warning of some event that would eventually take place in her waking life. The dream pattern escalated to incorporate this fear, so that she found herself waking into the dream, each time believing that it was actually happening.

My client regularly practiced visualizing different endings to the dream, replaying the new script until she felt at ease with a conclusion. All of her first solutions involved successfully calling out and having help actually arrive. In one early variation, it was a kitten who came to rescue her — that is, she was assisted by an aspect of the self that was feminine and cuddly, yet fiercely independent and able to care for itself. This solution made it clear that she was on her way to releasing and transforming the dream.

I have telescoped a longer sequence of dreams into these few examples. The process actually took place over a period of many months and included a number of variations on this basic theme. In the final stage of transformation, my client's dream reverted to its usual pattern. This time, as the door swung slowly open, she remained asleep and determined to see *what* was so frightening. It was a hairy monster. She looked at him carefully and concluded that he led a joyless life. Then she arose from her bed and invited him to waltz! The hairy monster was delighted to accept, and the bad dream melted away.

The invitation to dance seemed a brilliant resolution, and I was most impressed with my client's courageous struggle with her personal dream nemesis. She did say the hairy monster was not too light on his feet and annoyed her by stepping on her toes.

The general theme of this client's dream is actually a fairly common one. In her particular version, a hairy monster was the villain, although other clients of mine have encountered the frying pan man, the hot dog man, the balloon man, the homicidal maniac, and the Ku Klux Klan samurai. (The negative aspect of the self has many faces!)

Step 8:
Briefly Summarize the Dream's Meaning.

How Does This Apply to Your Waking Life?

In order to anchor and solidify successful dream transformations, it is useful to answer the question "How does this dream apply to my waking life today?" The energy released with dream resolution can trigger concurrent breakthroughs in waking life: Perhaps a new relationship will blossom, or you'll find greater satisfaction in work. A successful pregnancy, or even the end of a troubling marriage can result.

In my dream of Joan and my daughter April, I asked myself that same question: "How does this apply to my waking life?" I wrote, "I'm afraid that I am taking time to deal with what is important but secondary, while denying myself the time to care for what is of deepest value for me. I fear that this pattern will make me miss the boat of fulfillment."

The last thing I did was to draw in my journal two new sets of circles. Into them, I dropped the constellation of opposing traits that I observed in the two characters in my dream.

The diagram looked like this:

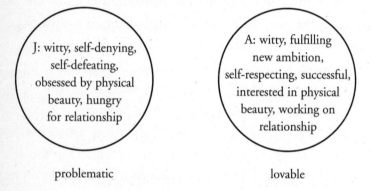

J: witty, self-denying, self-defeating, obsessed by physical beauty, hungry for relationship

A: witty, fulfilling new ambition, self-respecting, successful, interested in physical beauty, working on relationship

problematic   lovable

This step is an extension of the usual process. I used it to understand better what parts of myself were at issue in the dream. I then labeled one constellation of traits "problematic" and the other one "lovable."

My efforts at changing this dream were followed by a series of new dreams in which I was exploring and evaluating new living spaces. Looking up *Apartment* and *House* under images, I found the questions *What part of myself do I occupy?* and *What do I believe or fear about myself?*

Since Joan was often with me in my dreams, as I considered whether the house or apartment would do, I concluded that I was missing something about her that continued to be important and that I was actively working on in myself. What might her greatest problem be? The answer came immediately: Joan did not love or accept herself. This self-judgment she then projected to the world at large, with a terrible effect on her relationships with others — including the men in her life, family, and friends like me.

I concluded that by exploring new living spaces with a self-judging aspect of myself, I was giving time and attention to a part of me that I had ignored and possibly denied. With this understanding, the figure of Joan disappeared from my dreams. April continues to be a regular member of my personal cast, usually appearing in dreams in which I am examining professional choices.

Finally I went back to the issue of dream activities, which I had so conveniently skipped when I was first working with the dream in my journal. I was "swimming" with Joan, but was afraid of "missing the boat" that April was heading for. Swimming is associated with freedom and joy of movement in the water — the area of the unconscious and of emotion.

A boat allows safe and rapid travel over water. I concluded that it was relatively easy for me to take the time to explore the unconscious joyously. For example, working with my own and others' dreams is a great pleasure for me! More pleasure than work, in fact.

However, I was concerned about "missing" a more conventional means of travel. Some of my fears about not being successful must reflect my reluctance to go places by orthodox means. This connected with my daughter April, who has decided to follow a conventional mode of success by returning to college. I reassured myself that I can always dive off the boat for a refreshing dip in the sea of dreams!

Case History Using the Eight-Step Process

To review how to use the eight-step process for understanding your own dreams, I'd like to present a final case history: a vivid and meaningful dream experienced by a forty-three-year-old businessman who attended one of my Honolulu workshops in interactive dreaming. After processing the dream, he felt he achieved a significant personal breakthrough.

First I will quote his verbal report of the dream as he presented it during our workshop:

I am walking past the back door of my parents' house, where I grew up.

I look out the window, but see my reflection instead. I notice that I have an enormous erection and I'm nude. I look down at myself and see that I do have an erection, but it is nowhere near the size of the reflected penis.

I look back at the window thinking that it must be the type of glass that is making my penis look so big.

Now let me quote his written work on the dream as it appeared in his journal, with only minor editorial changes. His journal entry, using circles to diagram the dream, looked like this:

Step 1:
Record the images of your dream.

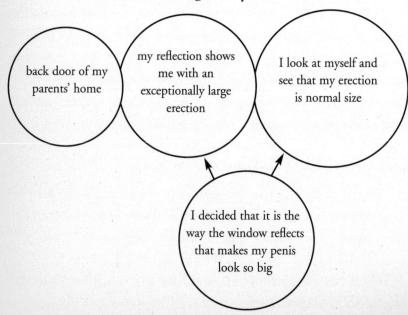

- back door of my parents' home
- my reflection shows me with an exceptionally large erection
- I look at myself and see that my erection is normal size
- I decided that it is the way the window reflects that makes my penis look so big

Step 2:
What word or phrase best expresses your feeling in this dream?

I am interested in the effect of looking bigger and more impressive produced by the back door window.

Step 3:
When is this same feeling present in your waking life?

In my awake life I have a similar feeling when the world perceives me as a successful businessman.

Step 4:
What were the significant activities in your dream?

I was observing myself, and, particularly, the "size" of my masculine attributes!

Step 5:
List the characters in your dream.
What part of you does each dream figure represent?

Just me . . . representing me!

Step 6:
List the significant places, objects, colors, and events in the dream.

My parents' house = the parental attitudes, beliefs, fears, and also the beliefs I grew up with and still hold unconsciously.

My erection = creative power. What do I want to do or make? I do want to make a "big" success of my business. I want to feel as successful as the outside world believes me to be.

Nude = Where in my life am I ready to be seen? I am ready to see myself as successful.

Back = Unconscious, "back there," what I can't see. I don't consciously agree with my parents, but the fears and beliefs are still back there.

The back door is a passage out with a window that lets me view where it leads. I get a reflection as in a mirror, which makes me ask: What am I ready to see? I'm ready to see myself as successful, which would be a passage out of my parents' beliefs about limitations and success.

Step 7:
What changes, if any, would you like to make in this dream?

I would like to walk through the door and participate in the larger world's view of me.

Step 8:
Briefly summarize the dream's meaning. How does this apply to your waking life?

This dream is about the limitations of my beliefs, particularly unconscious beliefs about success in the world. As long as I continue to hold my parents' point of view, my power will remain relatively modest, even though the reflection from outside (that is, from the world) is much larger.

This dream didn't feel very sexual, although I think my parents' attitudes about being careful — not "exposing" yourself, never taking chances — also apply to sexuality.

As long as I am in my parents' house (of limited ideas, ambitions, and beliefs about personal power), I won't really own the power that the outside world already reflects as belonging to me.

In his dream, this businessman felt he had successfully "uncovered" feelings that had been limiting his *experience* of professional success, even though others saw him as already being successful.

Some weeks later, he reported another dream:

While preparing to make a journey that would lead to my death, I was looking over some treasured items that I intended to bequeath to family members.

As he worked with this extremely powerful dream, he concluded that the part of himself that was preparing to "die" was the outgrown self who had accepted his parents' fears. By bequeathing to younger family members the "treasures" he had accumulated, he hoped to leave behind a more expansive and secure vision than the one he had inherited. After processing this second dream, he believed that he had successfully transformed the old fears and reservations about success that had burdened his family for years, perhaps even for generations.

As this businessman discovered, actively engaging in dream transformation will increase your feeling of command over waking-life events. Instead of being the victim of circumstances, you become a creative participant — shaping inner and outer circumstances to fit your deepest wishes and desires.

PART TWO

Basic Dream IMAGES

☾ Comments

All the items included in this index are organized alphabetically. But because it is often helpful to read over the associations for related items, there are several categories where, for easier reference, I have grouped together closely related images under subheadings. These categories include

Animals, domestic	*Clothing*	*House*	*Vehicles*
Animals, wild	*Colors*	*Numbers*	*Water*
Body parts	*Elements*	*Sex*	

All the items in these categories are also listed individually, in their proper alphabetical places. For example, if your dream features the image of a dripping faucet, look up *Water*. You will find the subheading *dripping*, along with more information about the different meanings for water and emotion in dreams. These additional associations and questions will often help you relate that single dream to a much larger dream sequence.

Image	Associations	Ask Yourself
Abandonment	Isolation. Leaving behind an old self. Release from control of old self.	What part of me am I ready to leave behind?
Aborigine See also **Native**.	Intuitive self. Magical identity. Primordial wisdom.	Where in my life do I seek alignment with natural forces?
Abortion	Loss of the new. Failure to nurture.	What part of myself do I feel is too weak to survive?
Above	Higher self. Greater understanding or knowledge.	What do I aspire to? What do I want to know?
Abuse	Fear-induced violence.	What fears do I hide with anger?
Abyss	Vast depth. Profundity. Infinity.	What lies deep within me?
Accident	Unexpected change. Upset.	Where am I avoiding change?
Acting/Actor	Role. Desire for recognition.	What role am I playing? Do I feel unrecognized?
Addict/Addiction	Obsessive need. Lack of control.	What habit is a threat to me?

Image	Associations	Ask Yourself
Adolescent	Lusty stage of development. Rapid growth. Immaturity.	What part of me is almost there? Where in my life is my growth most intense?
Adopting *See also* **Foundling; Orphan.**	Work on creative production.	What is being born in me against all odds?
Adult	Maturity. Wisdom. Full size.	What part of me has grown up?
Affair *See also* **Sex.**	Surrender. Ardor.	What do I wish to yield to?
African American	Freedom from repression.	In what way am I ready to be more expressive and creative?
After	Behind. In back of.	Where do I wish to move ahead? What have I created over time?
Agreement	If good agreement, harmony and commitment. If bad, compromise.	What do I wish to resolve? What am I willing to settle?
Ahead	In advanced position, in front.	Where am I ready to move forward?
AIDS *See also* **Plague.**	Hopelessness. Self-denial or guilt. Dependency.	Am I ready to stop condemning myself and others?

Image	Associations	Ask Yourself
Air See also **Elements;** **Wind.**	Breath. Intelligence. Force of mind.	What area of my life requires stimulation?
Air-conditioning See also **Air; Freeze.**	Purification. Relief or aggravation.	What do I need to breathe freely? Do I need to cool off?
Airport See also **Crossroad.**	Opportunity for rapid movement.	Where am I ready to fly?
Alabaster	Ornamental purity. Sometimes fragile.	What do I value for its delicacy?
Alchemy/Alchemist See also **Mage.**	Balance of elements. Transformation.	What magical metamorphosis am I ready to perform?
Alcohol	Relaxation. Indulgence. Freedom from responsibility.	What do I want to release?
Alert	Watching carefully. Ready.	What do I want to happen? Or what do I fear will happen?
Alien See also **UFO.**	Distant, strange, or unrecognized. Nonhuman.	What part of me is strange or unconventional?
Alive	Vitality. Existence.	What do I want to sustain?

Image	Associations	Ask Yourself
Alley	Life's passage. A narrow or secret way.	What choices am I ready to make public?
Alligator See also **Animals, wild.**	Primordial fear.	What elemental fears am I feeling?
Alone	Solitude. Retreat.	What part of me is isolated?
Altar	Holiness. Sacrifice.	What do I worship? Do I want to give something up?
Ambulance	Rescue. Swift response.	What part of myself wants to save or be saved?
America/American	Vigor. Ingenuity. The New World. Innocence or naïveté. Patriotism.	What am I exploring? What new world lies within me?
Anal sex See also **Sex.**	Submission. Union without issue.	To what or to whom do I want or fear to yield?
Ancestor	Inherited traits.	What qualities do I wish to preserve or be free of?
Anchor	Security. Stability.	Where in my life do I wish to hold fast?
Androgynous See also **Female; Male.**	Neuter. Union of opposites.	Where do I seek integration?

Image	Associations	Ask Yourself
Angel	Transcendent knowledge. Compassion. Higher consciousness. Revelation.	What inspiration am I ready to receive?
Animals, domestic *See also subheadings.*	The natural self tamed by civilizing values.	What part of me is ready to be tamed? Or wishes it were not so domesticated?
— *bull*	Fertility and strength. Rage.	What incites my passion?
— *calf*	Immaturity. Callowness. Youthful inexperience.	What qualities do I wish to develop? When am I ready to grow up?
— *camel*	Ship of the desert. Endurance.	What emotional resources am I conserving?
— *cat*	A feminine aspect. Cuddly and soft. Also independent and able to care for itself.	How am I integrating the yielding and independent parts of my nature? How do I feel about these qualities combined in a woman?
— *colt*	Potential. Gawkiness. Charm.	Where in my life am I beginning to realize my potential?

Image	Associations	Ask Yourself
— *cow*	Docile and productive. Nurturing, if passive aspect of self.	Am I passive? What do I nurture?
— *dog*	Usually a masculine aspect. Unconditional love. Obedient, loyal, trustworthy.	Am I trustworthy? What do I love unconditionally?
— *donkey*	Simplicity. Sturdiness.	Where in my life can I express my strength more directly?
— *goat*	Lusty vigor. Relentless energy. Omnivorous.	What am I determined to do?
— *goose*	Silly. Aggressive. Watchful.	Am I silly? Where in my life is my aggression apt to break out?
— *guinea pig*	Fecundity. Responsibleness.	What am I learning to care for?
— *hamster*	Dependency. Cuteness.	What part of me needs to be cared for?
— *horse* See also Vehicles.	Swift. Usually elegant. Feeling of developed consciousness. Sometimes unexpressed sexuality.	How do I feel about my power? What natural force am I suppressing or expressing?
— *horse, flying or winged*	Soaring consciousness. Limitless nature of self.	What part of me is ready to soar?

Image	Associations	Ask Yourself
— *lamb*	Innocence. Sweetness.	Where in my life do I wish to be gentle?
— *mule*	Obstinate. Intractable. Stamina.	Where in my life am I ready to persevere?
— *ox*	Burden. Strength. Stupidity.	How do I doubt my own strength? What makes me feel stupid?
— *pet*	Work on self-love.	What part of myself do I care for?
— *pig*	Greedy. Smart. Sometimes slovenly, sometimes fastidious.	Am I grabbing more than I need or can use? Did I clean up my own mess?
— *rabbit*	Fertility. Luck. Insecurity.	Where in my life am I ready to be productive?
— *sheep*	Conformity.	What am I following?
— *talking animal*	Magical communication. Natural wisdom.	What part of my nature has a message for me?
— *toy animal*	Playful relationship with the natural world. Freedom from responsibility.	Where do I want more pleasure in my life?
Animals, wild *See also subheadings.*	Natural, untamed self. Freedom from civilization.	What part of me seeks free expression?

Image	Associations	Ask Yourself
— *alligator*	Primordial fear.	What elemental fears am I feeling?
— *ape*	Dexterity. Mischief. Humor.	What part of me is almost human?
— *armadillo*	Armoring. Codependency.	What boundaries do I want or need to establish?
— *bat*	Nocturnal. Eerie. Keenly sensitive.	What darkness am I ready to navigate or explore?
— *bear*	Possessive love.	How am I threatened by love?
— *buffalo*	Boldness. Awesome strength. Pushy.	Where am I ready to be more powerful?
— *chipmunk*	Charming. Cute.	When am I friendly and wild?
— *coyote*	Trickster. Rogue. Thief.	What adventures do I seek?
— *deer*	Gentle beauty. Timidity.	What part of me hunts for protection?
— *dinosaur*	Fantasy. The power of size.	What part of me wants to be larger?
— *dolphin*	Natural intelligence. Transcendent wisdom. Compassion. Playfulness.	What part of me is divinely wise and playful?

Image	Associations	Ask Yourself
— *dragon*	Mastery of elements. Abundance. Matter and spirit combined.	In what ways am I ready to align the physical and spiritual aspects of my nature?
— *elephant*	Wisdom. Memory. The power of persistence.	Where does my wisdom lie?
— *fox*	Cleverness. Cunning.	What do I trust, or not trust, in myself?
— *frog*	Transformation.	What beauty lies within me?
— *giraffe*	Overview. Shy grace.	Where in my life am I ready to extend my vision?
— *gorilla*	Strength. Innocence. Rarity.	In what areas of my life am I ready to be strong and gentle?
— *hippopotamus*	Vast strength. Hidden danger. Size.	How do I conceal my power?
— *lion*	Nobility. Strength. Pride.	Where does courage dwell in me?
— *lizard*	Cold-blooded. Reptilian.	Where in my life am I ready to show more warmth?
— *monkey*	Dexterity. Mischief. Humor.	What part of me is almost human?

Image	Associations	Ask Yourself
— *mouse*	Meek nature. Quiet. Minor problems. Inner feelings. Shyness.	What small troubles are gnawing away at me?
— *opossum*	Feigning death.	What threatens me? Where am I ready to come to life?
— *panther*	Wild beauty. Grace.	What force do I wish or fear to unleash?
— *rabbit*	Fertility. Luck. Insecurity.	Where in my life am I ready to be productive?
— *raccoon*	Cleverness. Ingenuity.	What trouble am I getting into?
— *rat*	Street smarts. Clever. Sneaky and untrustworthy.	Where in my life do I fear betrayal? Can I trust myself?
— *rhinoceros*	Blind strength. Armoring.	What am I ready to see or understand about my power?
— *seal*	Comic instinct. Playfulness.	Where do I seek more joy in life?
— *skunk*	Passive aggression.	Where in my life do I feel the need to protect myself?
— *slug*	Work on laziness. Lack of charm.	Where do I want to take action? What do I judge in myself?

Image	Associations	Ask Yourself
— *snake*	Energy. The serpent power of kundalini. Sexuality.	What energy am I ready to express or understand?
— *squirrel*	Hoarding. Running in place.	Where in my life am I ready to feel more secure?
— *tiger*	Power. Wild beauty. Sexual force.	What is dangerous in me?
— *toad*	Infectious ugliness.	How or why have I concealed my true beauty?
— *toy wild animal*	Playful relationship with what is wild. Trust.	In what areas of my life am I ready to trust?
— *turtle*	Protection. Perseverance.	Where in my life do I feel safe when I take my time?
— *walrus*	Massive sensitivity.	Where in my life am I ready to be less threatening?
— *whale*	Power of the unconscious. Truth and strength of inner being.	What great truth am I ready to accept?
— *wolf*	Instinct. Appetite. Threat. Loyalty.	What instincts are a threat to me? What are my instinctive loyalties?
— *yeti*	Man-beast. Legendary.	What part of my greater self is stalking me?

Image	Associations	Ask Yourself
— *zoo animal*	Wildness under control.	What instincts do I want to observe or enjoy in safety?
Ankle See also **Body parts.**	Support. Direction.	Where am I going?
Ant	Social organization. Order. Industry.	How must I cooperate to achieve my desires?
Antique	Age. Survival value.	What part of me improves with age?
Anus See also **Body parts.**	Elimination.	What do I want to get rid of?
Apartment See also **House.**	A part of the total house of self.	What part of myself do I occupy?
Ape See also **Animals, wild.**	Dexterity. Mischief. Humor.	What part of me is almost human?
Applause	Recognition. Acclaim.	Where am I ready to acknowledge myself or to seek acknowledgment?
Aquarium	Microcosm of emotion.	What feelings am I ready to display or to view?
Arch	Fulfillment of aspirations. Higher goals.	What direction is opening before me?
Archangel See also **Angel.**	The power of transcendent knowledge and compassion.	What spiritual power am I ready to express?

Image	Associations	Ask Yourself
Archaeology	Rediscovery of the past.	What ancient knowledge do I want to recover?
Architect	Work on design of new self or identity.	What plans am I making?
Arctic See also **Frozen; Ice; North; Snow.**	Purity. Isolation. Frozen feelings.	What is frozen or melting within me?
Arguing	Verbal conflict.	Where do I hope for resolution?
Aristocrat	Noble or false status.	What privilege do I seek or deserve?
Arm See also **Body parts.**	Strength. To be prepared.	What am I ready for or getting ready for? What am I ready to give or receive?
Armadillo See also **Animals, wild.**	Armoring. Codependency.	What boundaries do I want or need to establish?
Army See also **Soldier; War.**	Organization. Cooperation for defense or aggression.	Where do I want to gather my forces?
Arousal See also **Sex.**	Stimulation. Availability.	What do I want to respond to?
Arrest	Enforced stop. Being caught.	Why do I fear being caught? What do I want to stop?

Image	Associations	Ask Yourself
Arrow	Hitting the mark. Cupid's dart. Painful realization.	What is the point?
Arson See also **Fire.**	Destructive rage. Cleansing anger.	What must I burn away in order to be free?
Art	Image of reality. Value. Creativity.	How do I express myself? What do I value?
Art gallery	Creative display.	What is uniquely mine? What am I ready for the world to view?
Artist	Work on creativity and originality.	What part of me is ready for expression? Where am I unique?
Ashes	Remains.	What is over for me? What am I ready to discard?
Asia/Asian	Wisdom. Subtlety. Inscrutability.	Where does my wisdom lie? What do I keep to myself?
Asphalt	Facility of movement.	Where do I want to go more comfortably?
Assistant	Giving aid or support.	What part of myself is ready to be called on?
Asthma	Loss of emotional security.	What part of myself am I preparing to care for?

Image	Associations	Ask Yourself
Athlete	Work on physical energy. Strength. Skill. Honor.	What abilities do I want to develop or be recognized for?
Atom	Essence. The power of the small.	What minute thing is of great importance to me?
Atom bomb	Destruction on a vast scale.	What am I ready to end? What do I fear is ending?
Attack See also **Fight**.	Violent change.	What conflict must I resolve?
Attention	Focused awareness.	What do I need to observe carefully?
Attic See also **House**.	Higher consciousness. Memory. Stored-up past.	What is "up there" that I want — or fear — to explore?
Attorney	Advocacy. Resolution of conflict.	Where in my life do I need help? What issues am I ready to resolve?
Auction	Public determination of worth.	What do I over- or undervalue?
Audience	Appreciation or criticism of performance.	What am I ready to make public?
Authorities	Commanding. Decisive.	Why do I desire or fear to be a leader?

Image	Associations	Ask Yourself
Autopsy	Seeing with one's own eyes.	What is hidden inside?
Avalanche	Catastrophic release of unexpressed emotion.	What old emotions are about to break away forcefully?
Award See also **Prize**.	Recognition. Doing it well.	What do I deserve?
Axe	Powerful severing.	What am I ready to chop away?
Baby See also **Blue baby**.	Infant self. Rebirth. Trust.	What is being born or reborn in me? What do I trust?
Baby-sitter	Work on inner child.	How am I preparing to care for the child inside of me?
Back See also **Body parts**.	Unconscious. "Back there."	What is going on that I can't see?
Backpack	Easy-to-carry opinions or responsibilities. Survival.	What can I conveniently carry? How well do my beliefs fit together?
Backpacking See also **Camping**.	Work on self-sufficiency.	What can I do without? What must I carry with me to survive?

Image	Associations	Ask Yourself
Bag	Small burdens. Convenience.	What minor responsibilities require my attention?
Baggage *See also* **Luggage.**	Opinions. Attitudes. Material goods and responsibilities.	What am I carrying with me? How do I feel about the load?
Bag lady *See also* **Bum.**	Insecurity. Failure. Loss of identity.	In what way is my identity or success threatened?
Balcony	Viewing. Seeing or being seen.	What do I wish to safely observe? How do I choose to be seen?
Bald *See also* **Hair.**	Sexual issues. Wisdom.	What do I want to give up, or fear to lose?
Ball	Integration. Wholeness.	What parts of my being am I uniting?
Ballet *See also* **Dancing.**	Disciplined grace. Culture.	Where in my life is my strength taking form? How do I wish to express it?
Ball game *See also* **Sports.**	Integration of individual and collective consciousness. Wholesome competition.	What do I want to be a part of? What group am I aligning myself with?

Image	Associations	Ask Yourself
Balloon	Lightheartedness. Joyfulness.	What makes my spirits rise?
Bamboo	Versatility. Exuberant growth. Strength. Flexibility.	Where in my life am I ready to flourish? What boundaries have I overstepped?
Bandage	Protection. Desire for healing.	What part of me am I ready to heal or take care of?
Bandit	Threat of loss.	What am I ready or afraid to give up?
Bank	Preservation of resources.	What do I want to save or to keep secure?
Bankrupt	Destruction of resources.	What must I protect to be secure?
Banquet	Formal celebration. Recognition.	What acknowledgment do I need to feel nourished?
Bar See also **Tavern.**	Relaxation. Indulgence. Irresponsibility. Pleasure.	Where in my life do I feel overloaded or stressed out?
Bark See also **Skin; Tree.**	Outer covering. Protection.	How can I find the balance between oversensitivity and insensitivity?

Image	Associations	Ask Yourself
Barn	Storage. Home to animal nature.	What part of me needs to feel cared for or safe?
Barrel	Containment. Capacity.	What am I storing? How much can I hold?
Basement See also **House.**	Below. The unconscious.	What part of my unconscious is ready to be seen?
Basket	Pliability. Craftsmanship.	Where in my life must I be flexible in order to carry on?
Bastard	Not genuine. Illegitimate.	Where am I ready to claim my heritage?
Bat See also **Animals, wild.**	Nocturnal. Eerie. Keenly sensitive.	What darkness am I ready to navigate?
Bath/Bathing	Cleansing. Release.	What do I want to wash away?
Bathing suit See also **Bikini; Clothing; Swimming; Water.**	Uncovered. Confidence.	What feelings am I ready to disclose?
Bathroom See also **House.**	Place of cleansing and release.	What am I ready to let go of?
Battery	Resource. Stored-up energy.	What do I need to recharge? What resource protects me?

Image	Associations	Ask Yourself
Battle *See also* War.	Conflict. Struggle.	What parts of me are at war?
Bay *See also* Harbor; Water.	Shelter. Enclosure.	Where do I feel calm?
Beach	Where conscious and unconscious meet.	What am I ready to be conscious of?
Bear *See also* Animals, wild.	Possessive love.	How am I threatened by love?
Beard	Authority. Power. Wisdom.	How do I express power? How is my authority shown? What am I hiding behind?
Beatnik	Rejection of social values. Isolation.	In what ways am I willing to stand alone?
Beautiful	Perfection. Realized ideal.	What do I admire or seek to become?
Bed	Sleep. Rest. Retreat from activity. Foundation.	What do I wish to retreat or rest from?
Bedroom *See also* House.	Privacy. Rest. Intimacy.	What is my inner reality?
Bee	Activity. Productivity. Social life.	Where in my life do I get a buzz?

Image	Associations	Ask Yourself
Beer See also **Alcohol;** **Drunk.**	Conviviality. Refreshment.	What do I need to relax?
Beggar	Lack of worth. Insecurity.	What is denied me? What do I deserve?
Beige See also **Colors.**	Neutrality. Detachment. Absence of communi- cation. Status.	What am I ready to take more seriously, or be less serious about?
Belching	Noisy release. Comic relief.	What can't I hold back?
Bell	Signal. Recognition. Celebration.	What do I want to hear or fear to hear?
Belt See also **Clothing.**	Holding up. Securing. Linking.	What am I ready to connect?
Bend	Not straight. Flexible.	Where am I preparing to yield?
Bestiality See also **Sex.**	Union with animal passions or instincts.	What basic aspects of myself do I fear or deny?
Bestseller	Great success. Achievement.	What do I appreciate or value in myself?
Bicycle See also **Vehicles.**	Self-propulsion. Recreation.	Do I have enough strength to make it? Will it be fun?

Image	Associations	Ask Yourself
Big	Larger than usual. Inflated. Generous.	Where in my life am I ready to expand? Where do I fear overexpansion?
Bikini See also **Bathing suit; Clothing.**	Exposure. Display. Revealing.	What am I ready to lay bare?
Bill	Payment due.	What has to be paid for?
Billfold See also **Clothing.**	Masculine security. Resources. Identity.	What feelings about security am I ready to change?
Bird	Freedom. Escape. Liberation from weight of physical plane. Spiritual forces.	What part of me wants to fly?
Birthday	Celebration of beginnings.	What is born in me?
Bite/Biting See also **Mouth; Teeth.**	Unexpressed fears around communication and nourishment.	Where do I need to take care of myself? What is after me?
Black See also **Colors.**	Isolation. Boundary. Separation. Introspection. Transition color. Peaceful.	What am I separating myself from?
Blanket	Comfort. Security. Warmth.	What discomfort or fear am I covering up?

Image	Associations	Ask Yourself
Blind	Unseeing. Unaware.	What am I ready to see or to comprehend?
Blinking	Blocking inner vision.	What do I fear to see?
Bliss	Ecstatic fulfillment.	What desires am I prepared to acknowledge?
Blocked	Fear of power or expression.	What am I preparing to clear or release?
Blond *See also* **Brunette; Redhead.**	Glamour. Artifice. Frivolity.	What part of me wants to enjoy life more?
Blood	Essence. Life energy. Threat to life.	Where in my life is my vitality spilling out?
Blouse *See also* **Clothing.**	Upper, as opposed to lower, self. Emotions.	What feelings do I consider appropriate?
Blue *See also* **Colors.**	Harmony. Spirituality. Inner peace. Devotion.	What is the source of my peace?
Blue baby *See also* **Baby.**	Weakness of trust. Threat to innocence.	What is feeble about my beliefs or faith?
Blue jeans *See also* **Clothing.**	Community. Comfort. Freedom.	Where in my life am I at ease? Where do I want to be more at ease?
Boat *See also* **Vehicles.**	Movement across the depths of feeling.	What emotions can I safely navigate?

Image	Associations	Ask Yourself
Body parts *See also subheadings.*	External form of internal nature.	What part is important?
— *ankle*	Support. Direction	Where am I going?
— *anus*	Elimination.	What do I want to get rid of?
— *arm*	Strength. To be prepared.	What am I ready for or getting ready for? What am I ready to give or receive?
— *back*	Unconscious. "Back there."	What is going on that I can't see?
— *brain*	Intellect. Mind. Reason.	What am I ready to understand?
— *breast*	Nurturing. Female sexuality. Maternal love.	What am I nurturing? What part of me needs to be loved?
— *buttocks*	Humility. Stupidity. Power.	Am I being an ass? What do I need to forgive in myself?
— *chest* *See also* Body parts: heart; lungs.	Fullness of life. Generosity.	What do I want to experience fully?
— *ear*	Receptivity.	What am I open to? What am I ready to hear?

Image	Associations	Ask Yourself
— *eye*	Vision. Consciousness. Clarity.	What am I aware of? How do I see the world?
— *eyelashes*	Protection of vision. Allure.	How well do I see? What can I safely observe? What do I show to the world?
— *face*	Identity. Ego. Self-image.	How do I appear?
— *finger*	Sensitivity. Awareness.	What am I touching?
— *fingernails*	Safe handling. Glamorous or functional.	What am I prepared to handle, or what do I wish to avoid doing?
— *foot*	Grounding. Direction. Basic beliefs.	Where am I going?
— *guts*	Fortitude. Stamina.	From what source do I draw my strength?
— *hair*	Protection. Attraction. Sensuality.	What am I covering? What do I display?
— *hand*	Capacity. Competence. Help.	What am I ready to handle?
— *head*	Intellect. Understanding. Superior.	What am I ready to understand?

Image	Associations	Ask Yourself
— *heart*	Love. Security.	Where in my life am I ready to give and receive love?
— *jaw*	Will. Relentless anger.	Where in my life must I dominate? Where am I ready to yield?
— *knee*	Flexibility. Humility.	Where in my life do I need to bend?
— *leg*	Support. Movement.	What supports me? Am I getting somewhere?
— *lungs*	Breath of life. Freedom.	In what ways is my life ready to expand?
— *mouth*	Nourishment. New attitudes.	What am I ready to take in? What am I ready to express?
— *muscles*	Power. Strength.	In what aspects of my life am I ready to be more powerful?
— *neck*	Flexibility, especially of vision.	What can I see if I make a small adjustment?
— *nose*	Instinctive knowledge.	How does it smell to me? What do I know without knowing?
— *penis*	Make sexuality. Yang power.	How is my power expressed?

Image	Associations	Ask Yourself
— *shoulders*	Strength or burdens.	What am I ready to carry? What is too heavy for me?
— *skeleton*	Work on support of structure. Remains.	Where in my life do I feel disconnected or falling apart?
— *skin*	Surface of the self. Sensitivity. Connection between inner and outer.	What is on the surface?
— *spine*	Support. Responsibility.	What holds me up?
— *stomach*	Digestion of information or circumstances. Understanding.	What value can I receive from my experience?
— *teeth*	Independence. Power. Ability to nourish and communicate.	Where in my life do I fear dependence? What do I wish to say?
— *testicles*	Yang power. Masculinity.	What power am I ready to express?
— *thigh*	Power of movement.	Am I strong enough to get where I want to go?
— *throat*	Communication. Creativity. Trust.	What am I ready to hear and say?
— *toe*	Beginning, especially of movement.	Where am I preparing to go?

Image	Associations	Ask Yourself
— *tongue*	The pleasure of taste.	What am I eager to try?
— *vagina*	Female sexuality. Yin receptivity.	What do I receive? What receives me?
Bomb	Explosive energy.	What is ready to explode?
Bondage	Restriction. Forceful limitation.	What am I afraid I might do?
Bone	Structure. Evidence. Support.	What supports me? Where do I look for support?
Bonfire	Joyful celebration of spirit.	What am I renewing?
Bonnet See also **Clothing.**	Sheltered or old-fashioned beliefs.	Where of how is my vision restricted?
Booing	Disapproval. Shame.	Where do I seek approval?
Book	Information. Guidance. Record keeping.	What am I trying to find out? Where am I looking?
Bookstore	Current information. Available knowledge.	What information am I shopping around for?
Boots See also **Clothing.**	Power of movement. Vigor.	What form of power do I seek?

Image	Associations	Ask Yourself
Border	Where two states, attitudes, or life patterns meet.	What new area am I preparing to cross into?
Boredom	Absence of commitment to ideals.	What is zestful for me?
Boss	Power. Direction. Control.	Where in my life am I ready or reluctant to take charge?
Bottom See also **Under.**	Foundation. Completion.	What have I explored fully? What do I wish to explore fully?
Boulder	Barrier. Building block.	What blocks my way? How can I use the material that has blocked my path?
Boundary	Useful or restricting limits.	What do I need to contain? What restricts my growth?
Bouquet	Acknowledgment. Adornment.	What recognition am I ready to receive — or occasion do I wish to honor?
Box	Enclose. Contain. Store.	What do I want to keep safe?

Image	Associations	Ask Yourself
Boxer	Work on power or confrontation.	What rules must I follow to be comfortable expressing my power?
Boxing	Strength. Power. Stamina.	Where in my life do I wish to be strong or assertive?
Boy	Yang power developing.	Where is power growing for me?
Boyfriend	Masculine ideal.	What do I admire in a man? What qualities am I ready to integrate?
Bra See also **Breast; Clothing.**	Private feminine self.	How do I express my femininity?
Bracelet See also **Jewelry.**	Binding. Commitment.	What do I wish to display?
Bragging	Insecurity.	What do I need to forgive in myself?
Brain See also **Body parts.**	Intellect. Mind. Reason.	What am I ready to understand?
Brakes See also **Vehicles.**	Control or slowing of movement.	Where in my life am I ready to feel more secure with my power?
Branch/Branches See also **Tree.**	Extension of growth. Natural shelter.	What direction am I growing? What protects me?

Image	Associations	Ask Yourself
Brave/Bravery	Boldness of spirit.	What dangerous risk inspires me?
Bread **See also** Food.	Sustenance. Shared resources. Uniting.	What fellowship nourishes me?
Breaking	Destruction. Forceful change.	What patterns or forms have I outgrown?
Breast **See also** Body parts.	Nurturing. Female sexuality. Maternal love.	What am I nurturing? What part of me needs to be loved?
Breath/Breathing	Spirit and measure of life.	What limits me? Where do I expand?
Bricks	Solidity.	What am I building to last?
Bride	Feminine receptivity.	What am I ready to receive?
Bridge	Connection. Overcoming problems.	What am I ready to cross?
Briefcase	Attitudes and beliefs about work and business. Professional identity.	How does my work fulfill or limit me?
Broken	Loss of usefulness or worth.	What am I ready to make whole or good?
Broker	Intermediary.	What do I want to negotiate?

Image	Associations	Ask Yourself
Brother	Masculine aspect of self. Fellowship.	What do I admire or fear in myself?
Brown See also **Colors**.	Material world. Security.	What needs organization in my life?
Brunette See also **Blond**; **Redhead**.	Sultry. Natural. Practical.	Where in my life do I want to be down-to-earth?
Bubble	Soaring. Release. Unreal expectations.	Where in my life am I ready to rise? Do I fear my expectations will not be fulfilled?
Bucket	Container.	What feelings can I easily handle?
Bud	Putting forth.	What is emerging from within me?
Buffalo See also **Animals, wild**.	Boldness. Awesome strength. Pushy.	Where am I ready to be more powerful?
Bug	Minor problems. Inconvenience.	What bugs me?
Build/Building	Inner and outer structure.	What do I want to give form to?
Bull See also **Animals, domestic**.	Fertility and strength. Rage.	What incites my passion?

Image	Associations	Ask Yourself
Bulldozer	Elemental changes. Bullying.	How am I transforming my connection to the physical world? What pushes me?
Bullfight See also **Matador**.	Formal ritual of death.	What danger am I ready to face?
Bum See also **Bag lady**.	Failure. Outcast. Loss of control.	Where do I feel I am losing control?
Bump	Sudden jarring. Wake-up call.	What disturbs or excites me?
Burial See also **Death**; **Funeral**.	Return to earth.	What am I ready to lay to rest?
Burning	Consuming energy. Fiery release.	Where am I most passionate?
Burst/Bursting	Forceful, sudden break.	Where is the pressure too great?
Bus See also **Vehicles**.	Shared journey. Mass transit.	How does my personal power relate to mass consciousness?
Busy	Fully engrossed in activity.	What distracts me?
Butcher	Carnivorous concerns.	What must I do to survive?

Image	Associations	Ask Yourself
Butter	Richness. Flavor.	What gratification am I hungry for?
Butterfly	Beauty. Freedom. Transformation.	What am I ready to change into?
Buttocks See also **Body parts.**	Humility. Stupidity. Power.	Am I being an ass? What do I need to forgive in myself?
Cage	Imprisoning of dangerous elements.	What part of me must I control or limit? In what ways am I dangerous?
Cake	Celebration. Sometimes treat, sometimes indulgence.	Do I deserve a treat? Can I indulge myself?
Calf See also **Animals, domestic.**	Immaturity. Callowness. Youthful inexperience.	What qualities do I wish to develop? Where am I ready to grow up?
Calm	Tranquility. Stillness. Dispassionate poise.	What makes me feel centered? Where have I achieved detachment?
Camel See also **Animals, domestic.**	Ship of the desert. Endurance.	What emotional resources am I conserving?
Camera	Image of experience. Record. Sometimes a means of distancing.	How does it look to me? Do I want to be involved?

Image	Associations	Ask Yourself
Campaign	Goal-centered commitment.	What am I for?
Campfire See also **Fire**.	Companionship. Shared energy.	What companions do I seek?
Camping See also **Backpacking**.	Natural living. Back to basics.	Have I denied basic needs? Am I well grounded?
Can	Preservation.	What do I want to keep?
Cancer	Destructive growth.	What part of me is out of control?
Candidate	Seeking responsibility or authority.	Where am I ready to step forward?
Candle	Illumination. Search for vision.	What do I want to see?
Candy See also **Sugar**.	Small treats. Temptation.	Do I receive what is essential to me?
Cane See also **Cripple; Crutches; Disabled**.	Limitation. Restriction.	What inhibits my free movement?
Cannibal	Part of the self sacrificed to the rest. Fear of integration.	What part of me is consuming?

Image	Associations	Ask Yourself
Canyon	A channel in the flow of consciousness. Passageway.	What feelings flow through me?
Cap See also **Clothing.**	Informal. Liberal opinions.	Where in my life do I want to be more tolerant?
Cape See also **Clothing.**	Dramatic protection. Fantasy.	What part am I playing?
Car See also **Vehicle.**	Personal power. Ego.	Can I get there? Who am I?
Cards	Skill and chance.	What game am I playing?
Carnival	Uninhibited fun. Freedom from restraint.	Where in my life do I want to cut loose?
Carpet	Protection. Insulation. Sometimes luxury or richness.	Where in my life am I ready to expand beyond my basic needs?
Cartoon character	Caricature.	What elements of myself do I find amusing or foolish?
Casino See also **Gambling.**	Risky business.	What do I hope to win, or fear to lose?
Castle See also **House.**	Fortified but noble self.	What walls am I ready to remove?

Image	Associations	Ask Yourself
Castration See also **Eunuch.**	Denial of sexuality. Limitation of creative power.	What is threatening about my creativity or my sexuality?
Casual	Uncalculated.	What is natural for me?
Cat See also **Animals, domestic.**	A feminine aspect. Cuddly and soft. Also independent and able to care for itself.	How am I integrating the yielding and independent parts of my nature? How do I feel about these qualities combined in a woman?
Catalogue	Opportunity. Options. Convenience.	What can I easily obtain?
Cave	Inner or hidden issues. Female sexuality. The past.	What is inside that I wish to explore?
Caveman/Cavewoman	Primordial aspect of self.	What is fundamental to my nature?
Ceiling See also **House.**	Upper limits.	Where in my life am I ready to raise my limits?
Celebrating See also **Ceremony; Party.**	Festive commemoration.	What do I appreciate or value?
Celebrity See also **Fan.**	Recognition. Fame. Sometimes notoriety.	What part of me wants to be recognized? Do I fear recognition?

Image	Associations	Ask Yourself
Cellular phone	Accessible, expansive communication.	What communication is of vital importance to me?
Cemetery	Death. Transformation.	What is over for me?
Centaur See also **Horse; Man.**	Union of animal and human nature, or of instincts and consciousness.	Where in my life am I integrating natural wisdom with intellect? What aspect of my sexual nature am I healing?
Center	Focus point. Quintessence.	What is my inmost nature?
Centipede	Poisonous feelings, thoughts, words.	What fears are restricting my progress?
Ceremony	Formal rite. Ritual.	What deep commitment am I ready to make?
Cesspool See also **Sewer.**	Accumulated negativity. Recycling.	What decision am I making?
Chad	Tiny piece on which much depends.	What am I filtering out?
Chain	Bonds. The strength of many.	What restricts or strengthens me?
Chainsaw	Forceful serving.	What must I rip apart or cut down?

Image	Associations	Ask Yourself
Chair	Position, style, or attitude.	What am I comfortable with?
Chairman	Authority. Leadership.	What rules do I follow?
Chalice	Inner wholeness. Spiritual self.	What spiritual thirst am I ready to quench?
Champagne See also **Alcohol.**	Celebration.	What do I wish to joyfully acknowledge?
Chandelier	Splendor of illumination.	What is my grand vision?
Channeling	Mediumship. Communication with higher realms.	What part of my greater self is ready to speak?
Chaos See also **Messy.**	Riot of potential.	What order am I seeking? What do I need to control?
Charismatic	Illusory magnetism.	What attracts or repels me?
Chasing	Pursuit.	Where in my life do I deny my power? What am I ready to catch?
Cheap	Of little worth. Good bargain.	What is valuable to me?
Cheating	Not right or fair, dishonest.	What must I make right?

Image	Associations	Ask Yourself
Check See also **Checkbook.**	Convenient resources. Safety.	How do I protect my resources?
Checkbook See also **Check.**	Available resources. Convenient money.	What are my available means?
Cherub	Divine innocence. Angelic child.	Where is my spirit reborn?
Chest See also **Body parts: heart; lungs.**	Fullness of life. Generosity.	What do I want to experience fully?
Chicken See also **Animals, domestic.**	Scattered, disorganized thoughts. Small fears.	Where do I need to focus my awareness? Am I needlessly fearful?
Child/Children	Innocence. The new self seeking to develop.	Where in my life am I developing? What part of my nature is childlike?
Chipmunk See also **Animals, wild.**	Charming. Cute.	When am I friendly and wild?
Chiropractor	Work on structure or support.	What part of me wants to be strong?
Chocolate	Gratification. Indulgence. Pleasure.	What do I want or fear to indulge in?
Choking	Restricted communication.	What am I afraid to say?

Image	Associations	Ask Yourself
Christ *See also* Jesus.	Higher consciousness. Salvation.	What part of me is divine? How do I experience my own divinity?
Christmas	Celebration. Holiday spirit of festivity and light. Reunion.	What am I celebrating? What do I wish to reunite with?
Church	Spiritual belief. Organized religion.	What is the structure of my belief?
Cigarette *See also* Smoking.	Stimulation. Addiction.	What do I seek distraction from?
Circle	Whole. Repetition. Infinity.	What is complete?
Circus	Childlike joy. Fantasy. Profusion.	What do I want to enjoy?
City	Civilized order. Culture. Community or decay of systems.	How do my parts cooperate or fail to cooperate?
Clapping	Approval. Encouragement.	What am I ready to appreciate in myself?
Classroom *See also* School.	Work on education or training.	What am I ready to learn?
Claw *See also* Animals, domestic; Animals, wild.	Threatening animal instincts.	What fears am I preparing to confront?

Image	Associations	Ask Yourself
Clay	Receptive matter.	What am I ready to form or mold?
Cleaning	Restoration of order. Purification. Maintenance.	What do I care for or what am I restoring?
Cleaning person	Work on disorder or wear and tear.	What needs my attention?
Cliff	Challenge. Precipitous height.	What do I aspire to?
Climbing	Aspiration. Growth with effort. Achievement.	What am I trying to reach?
Clinic	Detached attitude toward health and well-being.	What attachments are blocking my good health?
Cloak See also **Clothing.**	Magical protection. Secrecy.	What part of me is invisible?
Clock See also **Time; Watch.**	Timing. Measurement.	How much time do I have? What is running out?
Clone See also **Copy.**	Identical self.	What part of myself am I ready to see or know?
Close	Immediate.	What holds my attention?

Image	Associations	Ask Yourself
Closet	Storage of ideas or identity.	What is put away?
Clothing *See also subheadings.*	Identity. Self-image. Exploration of new roles or rejection of old.	What part of myself do I choose to show?
— *bathing suit*	Uncovered. Confident.	What feelings am I ready to disclose?
— *belt*	Holding up. Securing. Linking.	What am I ready to connect?
— *bikini*	Exposure. Display. Revealing.	What am I ready to lay bare?
— *billfold*	Masculine security. Resources. Identity.	What feelings about security am I ready to change?
— *blouse*	Upper, as opposed to lower, self. Emotions.	What feelings do I consider appropriate?
— *blue jeans*	Community. Comfort. Freedom.	Where in my life am I at ease? Where do I want to be more at ease?
— *bonnet*	Sheltered or old-fashioned beliefs.	Where or how is my vision restricted?
— *boots*	Power of movement. Vigor.	What form of power do I seek?

Image	Associations	Ask Yourself
— *bra*	Private feminine self.	How do I express my femininity?
— *cap*	Informal. Liberal opinions.	Where in my life do I want to more tolerant?
— *cape*	Dramatic protection. Fantasy.	What part am I playing?
— *cloak*	Magical protection. Secrecy.	What part of me is invisible?
— *coat*	Protection. Covering.	What am I covering up?
— *diaper* See also **Urine/** **Urinating.**	Untrained. Incontinence.	What loss of control may embarrass me? Am I being childish?
— *dress*	Self-image. Feminine self.	Who am I? How feminine am I?
— *garter belt*	Seductive support. Titillation.	What does it take to turn me on?
— *hat*	Opinions. Thoughts.	What thoughts or attitudes do I reveal?
— *helmet* See also **Clothing:** **hat.**	Protected opinions and attitudes.	What thoughts or opinions am I ready to change?
— *high heels*	Glamour. Restriction. Sexual invitation.	How comfortable am I with conventional femininity?

Image	Associations	Ask Yourself
— *jacket*	Freedom of movement. Adventure.	Where in my life do I seek liberty of action?
— *laundry*	Cleansing. Purification. Release.	What am I ready to clean up? What has been sullied through use?
— *overalls*	Common. Sturdiness. Protection.	What do I cover? What work is hard for me?
— *panties* See also **Clothing: underwear.**	Private self. Sexual identity.	What are my hidden feelings? What am I ready to expose?
— *playsuit*	Child aspect of self.	Where in my life do I want more enjoyment?
— *purse*	Feminine self. Sometimes sexual identity. Security.	What am I holding onto? What part of myself do I value?
— *shirt*	Upper, as opposed to lower, self. Emotions.	What feelings do I consider appropriate?
— *shoes*	General situations. Grounding.	How well do I connect with the world?
— *skirt or trousers*	Lower self. Passions.	What signals am I sending?
— *slip*	Private or inner self.	What do I wish or fear to reveal to the world?
— *socks*	Ordinariness. Comfort.	Where in my life do I want more ease?

Image	Associations	Ask Yourself
— *suit*	Formality. Professional identity.	What power or ability do I wish to be recognized for?
— *sundress*	Comfortable exposure.	What pleasures am I seeking? What part of me is ready to relax?
— *tights*	Shaping. Firming.	What can I safely expose?
— *underwear*	Private self. Sexual identity.	What are my hidden feelings? What am I ready to expose?
— *uniform*	Conformity.	Where in my life do I wish to share with others? Where do I want to break free of rules?
— *veil*	Illusion. Mystery.	What do I want to hide or to reveal?
Clouds	Transition. May be dark or light. Confusion.	What am I moving through?
Clown	Healing through laughter. Often bittersweet joy.	Must I suffer to be happy?
Club	Joining together. Fellowship.	What do I wish to belong to?
Clumsy	Graceless. Not smooth.	What am I ready to do easily?

Image	Associations	Ask Yourself
Coach *See also* **Carriage.**	Skilled training.	What do I want to learn?
Coal	Unrefined matter. Source of heat. Potential diamonds.	What potential lies within me?
Coat *See also* **Clothing.**	Protection. Covering.	What am I covering up?
Cocoon	Sheltered development. Safety.	What part of me needs protection in order to grow?
Coffee	Stimulation. Sometimes overexcitement. Communication.	What activates me? Where in my life do I need to slow down?
Coffin	Containing the end.	What am I ready to bury?
Coins	Small value. Lesser worth.	What is of significant value to me? Where in my life am I distracted by lesser concerns?
Cold	Emotional chill. Lack of circulation.	What warmth am I missing?
Colors *See also* **subheadings.**	Vitality, vigor, or lack of same.	What complex emotions am I experiencing?
— *beige*	Neutrality. Detachment. Absence of communication. Status.	What am I ready to take more seriously, or be less serious about?

Image	Associations	Ask Yourself
— *black*	Isolation. Boundary. Separation. Introspection. Transition color. Peaceful.	What am I separating myself from?
— *blue*	Harmony. Spirituality. Inner peace. Devotion.	What is the source of my inner peace?
— *brown*	Material world. Security.	What needs organization in my life?
— *gray*	Transition from one state to another. If clear, peace. If dull, fear.	What am I moving toward?
— *green*	Growth. Serenity. Healing through growth.	Where in my life am I growing?
— *orange*	Emotion. Stimulation. Healing.	What am I feeling?
— *pink*	Affection. Love.	To what am I responding?
— *red*	Energy. Vigor. Passion.	What is my source of energy or strength?
— *tan*	Convention. Hard work. Propriety.	In what ways do I seek or avoid respectability?
— *turquoise*	Healing. Good luck. Protection.	Where in my life do I feel safe?
— *violet*	Spirituality. Boundary between visible and invisible realms. Aristocracy.	To what do I aspire?

Image	Associations	Ask Yourself
— *white*	Purity. Clarity. Coldness.	What do I seek to purify?
— *yellow*	Vitality. Intellect. Clarity.	What do I wish to understand?
Colt **See also Animals, domestic.**	Potential. Gawkiness. Charm.	Where in my life am I beginning to realize my potential?
Column	Spiritual or historical significance.	What is of importance to me?
Comet	Messenger. Awakening or unleashing of energy.	What vision do I seek?
Committee	Delays or agreement.	What do I want to get done?
Commune	Collective energy. Socialization. Union of beliefs.	What do I wish to join? Who are my peers?
Compass	Knowing where you are.	In what direction am I heading?
Compost	Fertile refuse.	What richness is buried in my past?
Computer	Facility of communication. High technology.	What area of communication is opening up for me?

Image	Associations	Ask Yourself
Concentration camp	Fear and hatred of differences.	What is unique in me? What do I share with all others?
Concert	Work on harmony. Cooperation.	In what way do I want to join with others?
Condom	Sexual protection. Silliness.	Do I feel safe or silly about sex?
Confusion	Inner chaos.	What am I bringing together?
Connect	To bring together.	What is ready to be joined?
Constellation	Exaltation of light. Cosmic consciousness.	Where is my awareness expanding?
Constipation	Fear of letting go.	What am I holding back?
Construction	Work on structure of self.	Where in my life am I ready to build anew?
Contest	Competition. Rivalry.	What strengths am I ready to display?
Contraband	Forbidden desires.	What do I fear I can't have or don't deserve?
Convent	Spiritual community. Withdrawal from familial and worldly affairs.	What inner needs am I ready to nurture and support?

Image	Associations	Ask Yourself
Convertible *See also* **Vehicles.**	Glamourous power. Parade.	What power am I ready to display?
Cooking	Preparing to nourish.	What do I nourish in myself or others?
Copier	Repetition. Ease of reproduction.	What message do I want to circulate?
Copy	Duplication.	What do I want more of?
Corner	No escape. Hidden. Unavoidable.	Where are my choices leading me?
Corporation	Joining together.	What am I willing to be part of?
Corroding	Worn by age.	What have I lost?
Corsage	Ornament of honor. Recognition. Courtship.	What part of myself deserves or seeks to be acknowledged?
Cottage *See also* **House.**	Cozy, familiar house of the self.	What part of me wants to be snug?
Cotton	Natural comfort. Ordinary.	What puts me at ease?
Coughing	Need for attention.	What part of me needs to be noticed?

Image	Associations	Ask Yourself
Countries See also **Foreign.**	Alternative realities or attitudes.	Which of the qualities of this place do I find or seek in myself?
Country	Natural world. Space. Basic needs and desires.	Am I overcivilized? Do I feel confined by expectation?
Court	Resolution of problems. Conflict.	What issue am I ready to resolve? Where do I fear judgment?
Cow See also **Animals, domestic.**	Docile and productive. Nurturing, if passive, aspect of self.	Am I passive? What do I nurture?
Cowboy/Cowgirl	Adventure. Romance. Independence.	What part of me wants to roam free?
Coworker	Collaboration. Work on relationships.	How am I ready to be more cooperative? What is or isn't working for me?
Coyote See also **Animals, wild.**	Trickster. Rogue. Thief.	What adventure do I seek?
Crab	Soft meat, hard shell.	Am I too sensitive?
Crack See also **Drugs; Gap.**	Possibility.	What opportunity am I ready to seize?

Image	Associations	Ask Yourself
Cradle	Soothing. Safety.	How do I need to be cared for?
Crawling	Regressive movement.	In what areas of my life do I want to take my time?
Crazy	Total loss of control. Freedom from responsibility.	What holds me together? What happened if I lose it?
Credit card	Buy now, pay later. Ready access to resources. Protection.	What am I worth?
Creek 　*See also* Water.	The flow of feeling.	What feelings flow comfortably within me?
Creep	Self-judgment. Self-disgust.	What do I find loathsome in myself?
Crew	Collective ability.	Where do I seek community with others?
Crime	Guilt. Shame. Powerlessness.	What inner fear threatens me?
Criminal	Work on powerlessness.	Where in my life am I preparing to express my strength?
Cripple 　*See also* Disabled.	Disabled. Limitation.	What am I ready to heal?

Image	Associations	Ask Yourself
Cross	Sacrifice. Suffering. Salvation.	What do I wish to transform?
Crossroad	Choice of direction.	Which way do I want to go?
Crowd	Throng of alternatives. Options.	What are my choices?
Crown	Majesty. To be chosen.	What part of me seeks acknowledgment?
Crutches See also **Cripple; Disabled.**	Insupportable weakness.	In what area am I seeking freedom of movement?
Crying	Emotional release. Grief.	What emotions am I ready to express?
Crystal	Essential self. Clarity. Focus.	What is essential to me?
Cult	Unquestioning devotion. Sometimes obsessive beliefs.	Which of my beliefs are ready to expand? Which of my beliefs are limiting me?
Cup	Receptiveness.	What am I ready to receive?
Cupboard	Storage. Hidden.	What do I want to keep safe? What am I ready to disclose?

Image	Associations	Ask Yourself
Curtain	Protection. Decoration.	In what ways do I seek privacy? Or what do I wish to display?
Curve See also **Bend.**	Change of direction.	What is shifting for me?
Cuticles	Minor sensitivity.	Where am I overreacting?
Cutting	Separation. Division.	What must come apart?
Damage See also **Hurting; Broken.**	Injury. Loss.	What am I ready to restore or replace?
Dancing See also **Ballet.**	Joyous participation in life. Movement as transcendence.	What inspires me to go beyond my imagined limits?
Danger	Threatening change.	What am I afraid to lose if I change?
Dark	Mystery. The unknown and unformed. A place of fear or of potential.	For what do I search? What seeks to take form?
Dart	Point of awareness.	What hits the target?
Date/Dating	Courtship. Relationship.	What attracts me?
Daughter	Youthful feminine self.	In what area of my life am I ready to express youthful receptivity?

Image	Associations	Ask Yourself
Dawn	Beginning. Understanding.	What is beginning?
Day-Glo *See also* **Colors.**	Intensity of feeling or attraction.	What is alluring — or overwhelming me?
Dead	Complete. Over.	What has ended?
Deadline	The brink. Goal. Finish line.	What is driving me to completion?
Deaf	Work on communication.	What do I wish or fear to hear?
Death	End of a cycle.	What is over?
Debris	Fragments. Rubbish.	What do I wish to restore to wholeness?
Decaf	Avoidance of stimulation. Substitution.	Where do I fear over-stimulation?
Deck	Outdoor living. Connection between self and nature.	Where in my self do I seek alignment with nature?
Deer *See also* **Animals, wild.**	Gentle beauty. Timidity.	What part of me hunts for protection?
Defecation *See also* **Bathroom.**	Elimination. Dumping, especially of garbage from the past.	What am I ready to get rid of?

Image	Associations	Ask Yourself
Deformity	Failure of expectation. Disappointment.	What part of myself am I ready to accept and love? Where in my life do I seek perfection?
Delicate	Vulnerable. Exquisite. Slight.	Where am I tender? Where do I feel fragile?
Delicious	Attractive. Satisfaction. Fulfillment.	What delights me?
Demolition	Work on elimination.	What part of my life is no longer functional?
Demon See also **Devil**; **Monster**.	Image of self-doubt or denial.	What stands between me and greater consciousness?
Dentist See also **Teeth**.	Work on independence and power.	What part of me needs strengthening?
Depressed/Depression See also **Lonely**; **Sad**.	Suppressed emotion. Lack of options.	What am I afraid to feel?
Desert	Isolation. Retreat. Endurance.	What do I wish to withdraw from?
Designer	Organization. Form.	What new plans am I ready to formulate?
Desk	Organization. Getting down to business.	What am I ready to accomplish?

Image	Associations	Ask Yourself
Dessert	Indulgence. Treats.	What gives me pleasure? Where are my needs unfulfilled?
Detour	Change of direction in life's path.	What must I avoid to reach my true destination?
Devil See also **Demon.**	Negative forces. Temptation.	What lies between me and my own greater consciousness?
Dew See also **Water.**	Gentle release of emotion.	What feelings can I safely express?
Diamond See also **Jewel.**	Purity. Clarity. Enduring treasure.	What is precious to me?
Diaper See also **Clothing;** **Urine/Urinating.**	Untrained. Incontinence.	What loss of control may embarrass me? Am I being childish?
Diarrhea	Letting go.	What must I release?
Dictator	Control. Oppression.	In what ways can I be more flexible in making decisions?
Diet	Self-discipline or punishment. Self-restraint.	What must I give up or control to be healthy?
Dining room See also **Food;** **House.**	The ritual of eating. Formality.	What sustenance do I require?

Image	Associations	Ask Yourself
Dinosaur *See also* **Animals, wild.**	Fantasy. The power of size.	What part of me wants to be larger?
Dirt *See also* **Earth.**	If negative, unclean; if positive, fertility.	What do I need to clean up? What part of me wants to grow?
Disabled *See also* **Cripple.**	Restriction. Disadvantage.	What part of me is ready to be made whole?
Disaster	Great loss or suffering.	What changes frighten me?
Disc	Preserving knowledge. Receptacle.	What information do I want to keep safe?
Disguise *See also* **Hiding.**	Hidden parts of self.	What am I concealing? What am I ready to reveal?
Dishes	Vessels of nourishment.	With what am I preparing to sustain myself?
Dishonest/Dishonesty	Not according to the truth.	Where am I ready to come clean? What untruth must I confront?
Dismemberment	Pulling to pieces.	What must I pull apart in order to be together?
Ditch	Drainage. Escape.	What am I ready to clear away or escape from?

Image	Associations	Ask Yourself
Diving	Plunging into emotional depths.	What feelings am I ready to fathom?
Divorce	Splitting apart.	What commitment am I ready to end?
Dock	Safe landing.	What feelings have I safely navigated?
Doctor	Work on healing.	What part of me is ready to be healed?
Dog See also **Animals, domestic.**	Usually a masculine aspect. Unconditional love. Obedient, loyal, trustworthy.	Am I trustworthy? What do I love unconditionally?
Doll	Relationship practice.	In what area of my life am I ready to be more caring?
Dolphin See also **Animals, wild.**	Natural intelligence. Transcendent wisdom. Compassion. Playfulness.	What part of me is divinely wise and playful?
Donkey See also **Animals, domestic.**	Simplicity. Sturdiness.	Where in my life can I express my strength more directly?
Door See also **House.**	Access. Movement from one area to another.	What space am I ready to enter or to keep private?

Image	Associations	Ask Yourself
Dot.com	Communication. Visibility. Rapid development.	Where am I preparing to expand creatively?
Dove	Peace. Resolution of conflict.	What problem am I ready to solve?
Dowager	Imposing, if stuffy position.	Where do I feel limited by social expectations?
Down	Unconscious. Beneath.	What do I want to be aware of? What underlies my beliefs?
Drafted	Forced enlistment.	What am I forced to join?
Dragon 　*See also* **Animals, wild.**	Mastery of elements. Abundance. Matter and spirit combined.	In what ways am I ready to align the physical and spiritual aspects of my nature?
Dragonfly	Freedom and beauty of spirit.	Where in my life am I ready to fly free?
Drawing	Experience of life.	What is my vision of reality?
Dreaming	Creating. Waking to inner reality.	What is real for me?
Dress 　*See also* **Clothing.**	Self-image. Feminine self.	What am I? How feminine am I?

Image	Associations	Ask Yourself
Dresser See also **Cupboard.**	Storage.	What do I want to keep safe?
Dripping See also **Water.**	Trickle of emotion.	What am I releasing, bit by bit?
Driveway	Access to power and movement.	How easily can I access my power?
Driving See also **Travel;** **Vehicles.**	Work on energy and power. Life's passages.	How far can I go? What is my desired destination?
Drooling	Loss of control. Foolishness.	What do I take too seriously?
Drowning	Going under emotionally.	In what areas of my life am I ready to feel more emotionally secure?
Drugs	Healing or making insensible.	What do I want to stifle or to intensify?
Drum	Rhythms of life.	What beat moves me?
Drunk	Total insensibility.	Where in my life do I fear — or wish — to lose control?
Dry	Asceticism. Sterility. Preservation.	What do I wish to save? Where do I seek refreshment?

Image	Associations	Ask Yourself
Duck See also **Animals,** **domestic; Animals,** **wild.**	Amusement. Buoyancy.	How well am I adapting to my environment? What delights me?
Dummy	Representation. Emptiness.	What is missing in my relationships? What am I lonely for?
Dump See also **Garbage;** **Junkyard.**	Refuse of living. Elimination.	What do I no longer need?
Dune	Timelessness. Mutability. Flux.	Where in my life am I constantly shifting?
Dust	Aridity. Potential for growth.	Where in my life have I withheld the flow of feeling?
Dwarf	The power of the small. Unconscious forces. Magic.	What am I working to transform?
Dynamite	Explosive force. Sudden change.	What is ready to blow?
Eagle	Farsighted vision and power.	What must I understand to be powerful?
Ear See also **Body parts.**	Receptivity.	What am I open to? What am I ready to hear?

Image	Associations	Ask Yourself
Earth *See also* **Elements.**	Matter. Being grounded through nature.	How am I connected to the physical world?
Earthquake	Soul shaking. Deep levels of change.	What part of me is being shaken up?
East	Beginnings. Ancient truth.	Where am I heading?
Easy	Comfortable. Effortless.	What is natural and simple for me?
Eating	Sustenance. Satisfaction. Pleasure.	What part of myself do I nurture? What feeds me?
Eclipse	Darkening of the light.	What fears am I ready to behold?
Eel	Work on commitment. Slipperiness.	What threatens my freedom of movement?
Egg	Potential. Birth. Hopes. Wholeness.	What do I wish to develop?
Eight *See also* **Numbers.**	Eternity. Abundance. Power. Cosmic consciousness.	What am I willing to receive?
Election	Formal act of decision.	Who or what am I choosing?
Electrician	Work on energy or life force.	What part of me needs a charge?

Image	Associations	Ask Yourself
Elegant	Richness. Grace. Good taste.	What do I cultivate in myself?
Elements 　*See subheadings.*		
— air	Breath. Intelligence. Force of mind.	What area of my life requires stimulation?
— earth	Matter. Being grounded through nature.	How am I connected to the physical world?
— fire	Spirit. Energy. Unpolluted and cleansing.	In what areas of my life do I seek to be inspired or renewed?
— water	Emotion. Dissolving. Yielding. Release. Cleansing.	What am I feeling?
Elephant 　*See also* **Animals,** 　**wild.**	Wisdom. Memory. The power of persistence.	Where does my wisdom lie?
Elevator	Ascension. Increased understanding.	What am I doing to get higher?
Eleven 　*See also* **Numbers.**	Inspiration. Revolution. Higher octave of two.	What am I ready to change?
Elf/Elfin 　*See also* **Dwarf;** 　**Fairy.**	Playful otherworldliness.	What refreshes my spirit?

Image	Associations	Ask Yourself
E-mail	Casual, rapid communication.	What message am I sending or receiving?
Embroidery	Elaboration. Decoration.	What do I wish to embellish?
Emerald	Promise. Luxuriance.	What supports my growth?
Employment See also **Job.**	Occupation. Fulfillment.	What am I ready to do?
Empty	Containing nothing. Unloading.	What is gone? What do I want to get rid of?
Enemy	Denied self. Negative power.	What part of myself am I ready to transform and integrate?
Energetic	Power to accomplish.	What am I ready and able to do?
Equator	Rite of passage. Movement from one sphere of activity to another.	How am I becoming more whole?
Erection See also **Sex.**	Creative power. Fertility.	What do I want to do or make?
Eruption	Explosion of unconscious material.	What must I clear?

Image	Associations	Ask Yourself
Escaping	Getting away. Avoiding.	What part of myself pursues me?
Eunuch See also **Castration.**	Cutting off sexuality.	How can I be safe and sexual?
Europe/European	Culture. Old World. Preservation of the past.	What do I wish to continue or save?
Evergreen	Persistence in time. Unchanging.	What is eternal in me?
Exaggerate	Expand. Magnify.	What do I want to enlarge?
Ex-boyfriend	Masculine ideal, either integrated or rejected.	What have I accepted or failed to accept within myself?
Excrement	Elimination. Garbage from the past.	What am I ready to forget?
Execute See also **Judge.**	Punishment. Judgment.	In what area of my life am I ready to forgive myself?
Exercise	Flexibility. Strength. Stamina.	What new strengths do I want to take form? What am I building up?
Ex-girlfriend	Feminine ideal, either integrated or rejected.	What have I accepted or failed to accept within myself?

Image	Associations	Ask Yourself
Exhaustion See also **Tired.**	Squandered energy. Depression. Debility.	What feelings do I wish to avoid? What do I prefer not to think about?
Exhibitionism See also **Sex.**	Exposure.	What part of myself do I need to see or to understand?
Ex-husband	Male aspect of self, either integrated or rejected.	What have I accepted or refused to accept within myself?
Explosion	Sudden, violent change.	What is ready to burst forth?
Extension cord	Energetic connection.	What needs to be turned on?
Exterminator	Elimination of threat.	What weakness or strength do I fear in myself?
Extinct See also **Dead; Death.**	No longer existing.	What part of me has been annihilated?
Extramarital sex See also **Sex.**	Illicit union.	What is lacking in my relationship with myself?
Ex-wife	Feminine aspect of self, either integrated or rejected.	What have I accepted or refused to accept within myself?

Image	Associations	Ask Yourself
Eye 　*See also* **Body parts.**	Vision. Consciousness. Clarity.	What am I aware of? How do I see the world?
Eyelashes 　*See also* **Body parts.**	Protection of vision. Allure.	How well do I see? What can I safely observe? What do I show to the world?
Fabric	Substance of life.	What story am I weaving?
Face 　*See also* **Body parts.**	Identity. Ego. Self-image.	How do I appear?
Face-lift	Repair of self-image. Renewal. Vanity.	What part of my identity is ready for a makeover?
Faded	Used up. Tired.	What am I preparing to renew?
Fairground	Wholesome recreation. Festivity. Recognition.	What am I celebrating? What am I recognizing?
Fairy	Elemental being. Nature spirit.	What realms beyond the ordinary do I wish to explore?
Fall (season)	Cycle of transformation. Results.	In what areas of my life am I ready to benefit from my past efforts?

Image	Associations	Ask Yourself
Falling	Fear of failure. Loss of power. Loss of control.	Where in my life do I feel out of control? Where do I want to land?
Fame	Recognition. Notoriety.	For what do I seek recognition?
Family	Kin. Group.	What am I ready to relate to? What do I feel part of?
Fan See also **Celebrity.**	Admirer. Giving support.	What part of me wants recognition?
Farm	Domestication of nature. Sustenance.	What do I want to provide for myself and others?
Farmer	Work on relationship to nature.	What do I nurture in myself?
Farting	Defensiveness. Passive aggression. Failure to digest experience.	Where in my life am I ready to be more direct?
Fascinating	Irresistible attraction.	What am I drawn to?
Fast	Efficiency. Impatience.	Where am I in a hurry? What speeds me up?
Fat	Protection. Sensitivity. Safety.	What fears am I ready to lose?

Image	Associations	Ask Yourself
Fates	Destiny. Fortune.	What is inevitable? Or what do I hope for?
Father	Authority. Control. Guidance. Recognition.	What do I take care of?
Faucet See also **Water.**	Control or release of emotion.	What feelings do I turn on and off?
Fax	Contraction of space-time.	What am I ready to communication instantly?
Fear	Unexpressed love. Self-doubt.	What am I ready to accept in myself and others?
Feather	Effortlessness. Delicacy.	What is easy for me? What tickles my fancy?
Female	Yin. Fertility.	What do I want to reproduce?
Fence	Boundary. Separation. Where differences meet.	What am I fencing in or fencing out?
Fetus	Potential. Conceived but not yet brought to birth.	What do I wish to produce?
Field	Expanse. Area of activity.	What am I ready to cultivate in myself?

Image	Associations	Ask Yourself
Fight	Violent resolution. Release of energy.	What conflict am I building or releasing?
File	Records. Organization.	What do I wish to keep in order?
Films	The script or story being acted out. A means of distancing from events.	What is my story? What do I want to observe?
Finding	Discovery. Realization.	What am I ready to possess?
Finger See also **Body parts.**	Sensitivity. Awareness.	What am I touching?
Fingernails See also **Body parts.**	Safe handling. Glamorous or functional.	What am I prepared to handle, or what do I wish to avoid doing?
Fire	Spirit. Energy. Unpolluted and cleansing.	In what area of my life do I seek to be inspired, renewed?
Fireflies	Messages. Inspiration.	What quickens me to life?
Fireman	Protective masculine aspect of self.	What part of me needs to be rescued? What do I want to rescue?
Fireplace See also **House.**	Source of energy, heat. Spiritual center of self.	What is central to me? What warms me?

Image	Associations	Ask Yourself
Fireworks	Explosive festivity.	What is going out with a bang?
Fish	Emotion. Freedom of movement in element of feeling. Inner self.	What do I feel?
Fishing See also **Fish.**	Seeking underneath or inside for nourishment.	What do I hope to catch?
Fist	Threat.	What demands my attention?
Five See also **Numbers.**	Quintessence. Change. Celebration.	What is evolving in me?
Fixing	Restoration.	What needs to be repaired?
Flag	Patriotism. Identification.	What am I loyal to?
Flame See also **Fire.**	Inspiration. Intensity of emotion.	What feelings am I compelled to express?
Flasher	Frustrated sexuality. Exhibitionism.	In what ways am I denying my sexual needs or urges?
Flea	Inescapable minor irritations.	What old troubles am I ready to deal with?
Flirtation	Affectation of love.	Where or with whom do I wish to be intimate?

Image	Associations	Ask Yourself
Floating	Effortlessness. Buoyant.	What feelings support me?
Flood See also **Water.**	Overflow of emotion.	What feelings are too much for me?
Floor See also **House.**	Foundation. Basic elements.	Where in my life do I want to create stability?
Flower	Beauty. Sexuality. Blossoming.	In what ways are my beauty and sexuality blossoming?
Fly	Nuisance.	What annoys me?
Flying	Most common ecstatic dream. A joyous combination of control and freedom.	Where in my life do I feel this joyous power?
Flying fish See also **Fish.**	Freedom of feeling.	What experiences or emotions send me soaring?
Fog	Limited vision. Confusion.	Where in my life do I seek clarity?
Following	Pursuit.	What wants to be close to me? What am I ready to be close to?
Food	Nourishment. Security. Pleasure of greed.	What do I nourish in myself? What am I hungry for?

Image	Associations	Ask Yourself
Fool	Simplicity. Inanity.	What wisdom do I seek?
Foot *See also* **Body parts.**	Grounding. Direction. Basic beliefs.	Where am I going?
Footprint	Record. Memory.	Where have I been, or where am I going?
Foreign *See also* **Countries.**	Distant. Strange. Exotic.	What is boring about my life?
Foreigner	Expansion of self into unfamiliar realms.	What am I ready to explore in myself?
Forest	The realm of the unconscious. Natural forces.	What part of my inner nature am I ready to explore?
Fort	Defended self.	What defenses am I ready to examine?
Foundation *See also* **House.**	Basic principles or beliefs. Grounding.	What am I ready to make solid or secure?
Foundling	Abandoned aspect of self.	What part of myself am I preparing to care for?
Fountain *See also* **Water.**	Emotion springing forth. Freedom of emotional expression. Release.	What feelings are welling up in me?
Four *See also* **Numbers;** **Square.**	Stability. Matter. Strength. Worldly effort.	Where in my life am I most stable?

Image	Associations	Ask Yourself
Fox *See also* **Animals, wild.**	Cleverness. Cunning.	What do I trust, or not trust, in myself?
Freak	Abnormal. Unconventional.	What unique qualities am I ready to express?
Free/Freedom	Independence. Release.	What part of myself am I ready to liberate?
Freeway	Travel. Route to freedom. Movement.	Where in my life am I free to move?
Freeze	Emotional rigidity.	What feelings threaten my stability?
Freezer	Preserve. Chill.	What feelings are frozen within me?
Friend	Aspect of self ready integration.	What part of me is being integrated?
Frog *See also* **Animals, wild.**	Transformation.	What beauty lies within me?
Frozen *See also* **Water.**	Preservation. Restraint.	What rigid feelings am I ready to dissolve?
Fruit	Product. Offspring.	What am I ready to harvest?
Frying pan *See also* **Pan.**	Tool or weapon. Basic equipment.	What do I provide? How am I getting down to basics?

Image	Associations	Ask Yourself
Fuel *See also* **Fire.**	Warmth. Combustion.	What animates me?
Funeral	The end or death of something.	What part of me is ready to go?
Fun house	Amusement. Fear as pleasure.	What old frights am I beginning to find amusing?
Fur	Warmth. Luxury. Status.	What protects me or others?
Furniture *See also* **House.**	Identity. Attitudes. Beliefs.	How do I furnish the house of myself?
Future	Expectation.	What lies ahead?
Gaia	Protection. Source.	What nourishes or instructs me?
Gambling	Reward. Hope of recognition.	Where in my life am I ready to win?

Games
   See also **Ball game;**
   Sports.
	Life patterns. Cooperation. Competition.	What is important to me?

Gangster	Criminal. Rule of force.	What new rules do I want to establish for myself?
Gap	Absence of continuity.	What do I wish to join together or separate?

Image	Associations	Ask Yourself
Garage	Storage. Protection.	How do I take care of my power?
Garbage	Cleaning and clearing up.	What am I ready to get rid of?
Garden	Inner self. Growth or blossoming.	What do I nurture in myself?
Gardener	Natural process. Growth.	What is growing in me?
Garter belt See also **Clothing.**	Seductive support. Titillation.	What does it take to turn me on?
Gas station	Source of power.	What fuels me?
Gate	Threshold.	What invites me? What do I keep outside?
Gear	Ideas. Attitudes. Beliefs.	What do I value? What is useful to me?
Gentle	Tenderness. Peace.	What calms me?
Gestapo	Torture. Terror in the night.	What part of me seeks forgiveness?
Ghost	Spiritual aspect of self — sometimes feared. Memory.	What keeps coming back for me?
Ghoul	Death in life.	What part of myself threatens my survival?

Image	Associations	Ask Yourself
Giant	The power of size.	What inferiority am I ready to transform?
Gift	Recognition. Acknowledgment.	What part of myself do I wish to honor? What do I appreciate?
Giraffe See also **Animals, wild.**	Overview. Shy grace.	Where in my life am I ready to extend my vision?
Girl	Receptive or yin quality.	Where in my life am I learning to be receptive?
Girlfriend	Feminine ideal.	What do I admire in a female? What feminine aspect am I ready to integrate?
Glasses	Vision. Attitude. Belief.	What correction is necessary for me to see clearly?
Glue	Uniting. Repairing.	What is coming together for me?
Goal	Aspirations. Unfulfilled desires.	What am I ready to achieve?
Goat See also **Animals, domestic.**	Lusty vigor. Relentless energy. Omnivorous.	What am I determined to do?
Goblin	Apparition of fear.	What fears am I ready to examine or confront?

Image	Associations	Ask Yourself
God	Divine masculine. Sacred. Creator.	What do I hold sacred?
Goddess	Divine feminine. Compassion. Love.	What qualities do I worship?
Gold	Ultimate value. Splendor.	What do I treasure? What part of me has great worth?
Goldfish See also **Fish; Gold.**	Low maintenance. Impermanence.	What small things give me pleasure?
Golf	High-status recreation.	How can I enjoy increased self-worth?
Goose See also **Animals, domestic.**	Silly, aggressive, watchful.	Am I silly? Where in my life is my aggression apt to break out?
Gorilla See also **Animals, wild.**	Strength. Innocence. Rarity.	In what areas of my life am I ready to be strong and gentle?
Gossip	Unwelcome or harmless news.	What truth must I own?
Government	Administrative regulation. Control. Provider.	Where in my life do I feel controlled or taken care of?
Grace	Blessing. Rapture.	What is transcendent within me?

Image	Associations	Ask Yourself
Graduation	Completion.	Where am I ready to move on?
Grandparent	Gentle authority. Kindness.	Where in my life do I seek support?
Grass	Natural protection. Ubiquity.	What part of myself can I always rely on?
Gravel See also **Rock; Stone.**	Utility. Common.	Where in my life am I ready to be practical?
Gray See also **Colors.**	Transition from one state to another. If clear, peace. If dull, fear.	What am I moving toward?
Greedy	Unfulfilled desires or needs.	What am I starving for? What do I deserve?
Green See also **Colors.**	Growth. Serenity. Healing through growth.	Where in my life am I growing?
Groceries See also **Food.**	Nurture. Necessities.	What do I need to feel well supplied?
Grocery store	Source of provisions.	What am I ready to provide for myself?
Groom	Masculine activity and energy.	What union am I ready to commit myself to?

Image	Associations	Ask Yourself
Guarding	Shelter. Protection.	Where must I be vigilant, or where am I hypervigilant?
Guerrilla	Underground rebellion.	What part of me is in revolt?
Guest	Temporary association.	What part of myself do I want to know better?
Guilt/Guilty	Judgment. Absence of pride.	What am I ready to forgive in myself or in others?
Guinea pig *See also* **Animals, domestic.**	Fecundity. Responsibleness.	What am I learning to care for?
Gulf	Abyss. Enclosing vastness.	What boundaries do I seek?
Gum	Release of nervous tension.	What relaxes me?
Gun	Violence. Aggression. Threat.	What threatens me? Where in my life do I want protection?
Guru	Knowledge. Inspiration. Obsession. Devotion.	How do I wish or fear to be more powerful in the world?
Guts *See also* **Body parts.**	Fortitude. Stamina.	From what source do I draw my strength?

Image	Associations	Ask Yourself
Gypsy	Freedom from conventions. Mobility.	How does culture restrict or protect me?
Hair See also **Body parts.**	Protection. Attraction. Sensuality.	What am I covering? What do I display?
Hairdresser	Work on self-image and self-esteem.	What am I ready to feel better about?
Hall See also **House.**	Access. Privacy.	How well do the parts of myself connect?
Hammer	Construction. Striking out.	Where in my life am I building or tearing down?
Hamster See also **Animals, domestic.**	Dependency. Cuteness.	What part of me needs to be cared for?
Hand See also **Body parts.**	Capacity. Competence. Help.	What am I ready to handle?
Handle	Understanding. Usefulness.	What am I ready to make use of?
Handsome	Conventional ideal.	Where do I feel lacking?
Hanging	Holding back communication.	What am I ready to hear?
Hanging out	Ease. Stress-free.	Where do I need to relax?
Happy	Self-love. Contentment.	What have I accepted in myself?

Image	Associations	Ask Yourself
Harbor *See also* **Water.**	Shelter. Safety.	Where in my life do I find emotional peace?
Hat *See also* **Clothing.**	Opinions. Thoughts.	What thoughts or attitudes do I reveal?
Haunted house *See also* **House.**	Childhood fears. Prohibition. Past limitation.	What part of my past am I ready to purify or exorcise?
Hawk	Vision. Vigilance.	What is my highest vision?
Haystack	Playful concealment. Rusticity.	How am I burdened by sophistication?
Head *See also* **Body parts.**	Intellect. Understanding. Superior.	What am I ready to understand?
Headache	Painful self-image.	What am I ready to love and accept in myself?
Headline	Important. Significant.	What must I notice?
Healer/Healing	Restoration. Recovery.	Where in my life am I ready to be whole?
Hearing aid	Work on failure to communicate.	What am I preparing to hear?
Heart *See also* **Body parts.**	Love. Security.	Where in my life am I ready to give and receive love?

Image	Associations	Ask Yourself
Heart attack	Loss of love or acceptance.	Where in my life do I need to give and receive more love?
Heat	Intense emotion. Stress. High temperature or passion.	Where do I need to cool off or warm up?
Heaven	Bliss. Transcendence.	Where in my life do I feel blessed?
Heavy	Burdensome. Serious.	What am I strong enough to bear or ready to understand?
Hedge	Natural separation.	What do I choose to keep separate?
Helicopter See also **Vehicles.**	Movement in many directions.	Where in my life do I want more freedom of movement?
Hell	Torment. Spiritual agony.	What am I ready to forgive in myself or others?
Helmet See also **Clothing.**	Protected opinions and attitudes.	What thoughts or opinions am I ready to change?
Hemorrhoids	Painful letting go.	What must I be rid of?

Image	Associations	Ask Yourself
Herb	Savor. Subtlety.	In what way am I seeking more flavor from life?
Herpes	Misuse of sexual energy. Unwise sexual expression.	What worries me about sex?
Hiccup	Interruptions.	Where do I need to take my time?
Hiding	Concealment. Secrets.	Where do I need to feel safe?
High	Expanded awareness. Inflation.	What larger view do I wish to see?
High heels See also **Clothing**.	Glamour. Restriction. Sexual invitation.	How comfortable am I with conventional femininity?
High places	Attainment. Greater understanding.	What do I want to achieve? Where must I got to achieve it?
Hiking	Work on process. Advancement.	Where do I want to go? Am I strong enough to make it?
Hill	Easy achievement. Comfortable progress.	What is easy for me to do?

Image	Associations	Ask Yourself
Hippie	Freedom. Excess. Rejection of conventional values.	What part of me desires or fears to be different?
Hippopotamus See also **Animals, wild.**	Vast strength. Hidden danger. Size.	How do I conceal my power?
Hit/Hitting	Unexpressed anger.	What do I need to be grateful for?
Hit and run	Old guilt. Conscience.	What do I want to forgive in myself and others?
Hitchhiker	Freedom. Irresponsibility.	What part of me wants a free ride?
Hole	The beginning of change.	What is transforming?
Hologram	Totality. The part as equal to the whole.	In what way am I ready to see the perfection of my being?
Home See also **House.**	Center of being. Spiritual self.	Where does my spirit reside?
Homeless See also **House.**	Spiritual deprivation. Absence of security and stability.	What new structure am I seeking?

Image	Associations	Ask Yourself
Homosexual See also **Sex**.	Union — or fear of union — with aspects of self.	What part of my femininity or masculinity do I seek to merge with?
Honey	Sweetness. Attraction.	What pleasures lure me?
Honeycomb	Contained sweetness.	What pleasure do I want to hold onto?
Hoodlum	Frustration. Social rejection.	What do I wish to reform in myself?
Hook See also **Fishing**.	To ensnare. Trap.	What do I want to catch?
Hope/Hopeful	Core belief.	What sustains me?
Horse See also **Animals, domestic; Vehicles**.	Swift. Usually elegant. Feeling of developed consciousness. Sometimes unexpressed sexuality.	How do I feel about my power? What natural force am I suppressing or expressing?
Horse, flying or winged See also **Animals, domestic**.	Soaring consciousness. Limitless nature of self.	What part of me is ready to soar?
Hose See also **Water**.	Flexibility. Flow of emotion.	How well do I communicate my feelings?
Hospital	Healing. Confinement.	What am I ready to heal?

Image	Associations	Ask Yourself
Hostage	Imprisonment as security.	What do I get from holding myself or others back?
Hotel	Transitional aspect of identity.	What part of me is in transit?
House *See also subheadings.*	Being. The house of self.	What do I believe or fear about myself?
— *apartment*	A part of the total house of self.	What part of myself do I occupy?
— *attic*	Higher consciousness. Memory. Stored-up past.	What is "up there" that I want or fear to explore?
— *basement*	Below. The unconscious.	What part of my unconscious is ready to be seen?
— *bathroom*	Place of cleansing and release.	What am I ready to release?
— *bedroom*	Privacy. Rest. Intimacy.	What is my inner reality?
— *castle*	Fortitude but noble self.	What walls am I ready to remove?
— *ceiling*	Upper limits.	Where in my life am I ready to raise my limits?

Image	Associations	Ask Yourself
— *cottage*	Cozy, familiar house of the self.	What part of me wants to be snug?
— *dining room*	The ritual of eating. Formality.	What sustenance do I require?
— *door*	Access. Movement from one area to another.	What space am I ready to enter or to keep private?
— *fireplace*	Source of energy, heat, Spiritual center of self.	What is central to me? What warms me?
— *floor*	Foundation. Basic elements.	Where in my life do I want to create stability?
— *foundation*	Basic principles or beliefs. Grounding.	What am I ready to make solid or secure?
— *furniture*	Identity. Attitudes. Beliefs.	How do I furnish the house of my self?
— *garage*	Storage. Protection.	How do I take care of my power?
— *hall*	Access. Privacy.	How well do the parts of myself connect?
— *haunted house*	Childhood fears. Prohibition. Past limitation.	What part of my past am I ready to purify or exorcise?
— *home*	Center of being. Spiritual self.	Where does my spirit reside?

Image	Associations	Ask Yourself
— *homeless*	Spiritual deprivation. Absence of security and stability.	What new structure am I seeking?
— *hut*	Basic or primordial needs. Retreat. Humility.	Where in my life am I ready to be humble?
— *kitchen*	Nourishment. Productivity.	What's cooking?
— *living room*	Central space of the house of self.	What is central to my being?
— *mansion*	Expansive residence of the self.	What part of me needs more room?
— *palace*	Potential kingdom of the self.	How can I fulfill my potential?
— *porch*	Intersection of self with the world.	Where in my life am I ready to be more approachable?
— *rafters*	Protective support.	What supports my higher consciousness?
— *roof*	Above. Protection. Covering.	Where in my life am I ready to expand my limitations?
— *stairs*	Ascent. Going higher. Aspiration. Descent. Grounding.	What do I want to rise or descend to?

Image	Associations	Ask Yourself
— *wall*	Barrier. Defense. Partition.	What am I ready to integrate? What separation is necessary for me? What is on the other side?
— *window*	Vision. Seeing and being seen.	What am I willing to see? What do I wish to reveal or conceal?
Howl/Howling	Wounded feelings.	Where am I hurt? What old fears must I express?
Hugging See also **Sex.**	Loving appreciation. Acknowledgment.	What part of me needs more attention?
Humming	Outward expression of unconscious inner state.	What tune do I sing?
Hummingbird	Joyful freedom. Nourishing sweetness.	What makes my heart light?
Hunting	Pursuit. Search. Quest.	What part of my larger self am I ready to apprehend?
Hurricane	Destructive emotions.	What powerful feelings am I ready to experience?
Hurting	Work on old pains.	What wounds do I wish to heal?
Husband	Yang aspect of self. Partner.	What am I committed to?

Image	Associations	Ask Yourself
Hut See also **House.**	Basic or primordial needs. Retreat. Humility.	Where in my life am I ready to be humble?
Hydrofoil See also **Travel; Vehicles.**	Soaring above the sea of feeling.	What emotions no longer inhibit me?
Ice See also **Water.**	A rigid feeling state. Frozen.	What feelings are locked within or ready to be melted away?
Ice pick	Cold feelings.	What feelings are frozen in me?
Identical See also **Twin.**	Reflection.	What do I see in myself?
Idle	Freedom. Boredom.	What do I want to do or avoid doing?
Immobile	Terror. Resistance.	What fear prevents my growth?
Impeachment	Challenge to authority.	What exposure do I seek or fear?
Incense	Ritual. Atmosphere.	What influences my environment?
Incest See also **Sex.**	Fear of love.	Am I ready to be sexually mature?

Image	Associations	Ask Yourself
Infection See also **Sick.**	Threat from without.	What small thing troubles me?
Information	Knowledge. Belief.	What am I ready to be aware of?
Inheritance	Value from the past.	What am I ready to claim as mine?
Injection	Forceful introduction. Need.	What must I have?
Injury See also **Hurting.**	Work on old wounds.	What damage am I ready to repair?
Inspiration	High levels of feeling.	What elevates my consciousness?
Insurance	Absence of trust. Security.	What losses do I fear? How do I block my own progress?
Intercourse See also **Sex.**	Union. Release. Pleasure. Creation.	What do I want or fear to merge with?
Internet	Boundaryless communication.	What limits am I ready to transcend?
Invalid See also **Cripple; Disabled.**	Infirmity. Work on long-standing weakness or illness.	What old limitations am I ready to heal?
Invasion	Forced entry. Attack.	What part of me is ready to be more assertive?

Image	Associations	Ask Yourself
Invent/Inventing	Creative essence.	What is taking form within me?
Invisible	Loss of self. Dispassion.	What part of me wants to be seen? What can I observe without becoming involved?
Invitation	Union with others.	What or who do I want to join?
Iron	Rigidity. Steadfastness. Endurance.	Where in my life must I stand firm?
Irritable	Nervous overload.	What stresses me? What feeling am I avoiding?
Island	Solitude. Separation. Escape. May be enjoyable or lonely.	What do I separate myself from?
Jacket See also **Clothing.**	Freedom of movement. Adventure.	Where in my life do I seek liberty of action?
Jackhammer	Breaking up of old structures.	What course am I ready to change?
Jade	Protection. Good fortune.	Where in my life do I feel blessed or wish to be blessed?
Jaw See also **Body parts.**	Will. Relentless anger.	Where in my life must I dominate? Where am I ready to yield?

Image	Associations	Ask Yourself
Jealousy	Work on fear of intimacy.	Where in my life am I ready to show my vulnerability?
Jeep See also **Vehicles.**	Ruggedness. Utility. Efficiency.	Where in my life must I be sturdy to reach my goal?
Jellyfish	Spineless. Passive aggression.	Where in my life am I ready to express myself more forcefully?
Jesus See also **Christ.**	Human aspect of divinity. Salvation. Healing.	What part of me is ready to be saved?
Jewel	Treasure. Essence. Precious.	What is valuable? What do I value in myself?
Jewelry	Display. Wealth. Status.	What is my worth? How do I show it?
Job See also **Employment.**	Work on fulfillment.	Where in my life am I frustrated or satisfied?
Joint	Connection. Junction.	What is coming together for me?
Journey See also **Travel.**	Liberation. Movement toward inner center.	What is my inner process?
Joy	Gladness. Abundant well-being.	What have I accepted unconditionally?

Image	Associations	Ask Yourself
Judge	Decision making. Wisdom or condemnation.	What decision am I ready to make? What part of me is wise and knowledgeable?
Junk/Junkyard	Discarded ideas, attitudes, beliefs.	What value can I find in the past?
Jury	Informed consensus. Deliberation.	What decision am I contemplating?
Key	Solution. Access.	What problem am I ready to solve?
Kidnapped	Work on independence and freedom.	What responsibilities do I wish or fear to assume?
King	Noble aspect of masculinity.	Where in my life am I ready to express masculine power?
Kissing See also **Sex.**	Intimacy. Affection. Greeting.	What or whom do I wish to be close to?
Kitchen See also **House.**	Nourishment. Productivity.	What's cooking?
Knee See also **Body parts.**	Flexibility. Humility.	Where in my life do I need to bend?
Knife	Aggression. Serving. Anger.	What do I want to cut out?

Image	Associations	Ask Yourself
Knight See also **Nobility;** **Soldier; Warrior.**	Noble defense.	Where do I need protection?
Knob	Protuberance.	What sticks out? What am I ready to notice?
Knot See also **Knots.**	Bond of union. Entanglement. Complication.	What is connected in me? What do I want or fear to tie together?
Knots. See also **Knot.**	Restriction. Holding together.	What is tied up in me?
Ku Klux Klan	Secret terrorism. Prejudice.	What hidden fears or judgments am I preparing to confront?
Laboratory	Exploration. Detached examination.	What am I searching for?
Lace	Ornament. Delicacy.	Where have I been too practical?
Ladder	Reaching upward.	How high am I ready to climb?
Lake See also **Water.**	Contained emotion. Often a sense of tranquility or peace.	What feelings do I comfortably contain?
Lamb See also **Animals,** **domestic.**	Innocence. Sweetness.	Where in my life do I wish to be more gentle?

Image	Associations	Ask Yourself
Lame	Restricted movement.	What holds me back?
Lamp	Illumination.	What do I want to see more clearly?
Landscape	Scenic beauty.	What is beautiful about my nature?
Landslide	Work on emotional stability. Fear of change.	What old survival skills am I ready to drop?
Laptop	Portable communication.	What must I be able to communicate in any circumstances?
Laser	Focused awareness.	Where am I concentrating my understanding or ability?
Latino/Latina	Spontaneity. Relaxation. Volatility.	What do I wish to change? What part of me is impulsive?
Laughing	Communication of joy. Joyous release. Scorn.	In what way am I ready to lighten up? What pressure do I want to release?
Laundry **See also Cleaning; Clothing.**	Cleansing. Purification. Release.	What am I ready to clean up? What has been sullied through use?
Lawn	Control of growth.	What do I want to keep smooth and trim?

Image	Associations	Ask Yourself
Leaf	Receptivity. Growth.	What am I open to?
Leaping	Enthusiasm. Excitement. Action.	What am I eager for?
Leash	Control. Restraint.	What leads me? What am I attached to?
Leather	Eroticism. Adventure. Glamour.	What image am I creating?
Lecturing	Communication. Sermonizing.	What am I ready to hear or to say? What is my expertise?
Leech	Energy draining.	Where do I fear loss of life force?
Left	Emotions. The dark way. Intuition.	What feelings must I trust to feel safe?
Leg See also **Body parts.**	Support. Movement.	What supports me? Am I getting somewhere?
Lei See also **Corsage.**	Token of honor or affection.	What do I wish to recognize in myself?
Letter See also **Mail.**	Direct communication.	What am I ready to say or to hear?
Lever	Purchase. Take charge.	What do I want to maneuver?

Image	Associations	Ask Yourself
Library	Knowledge. Records. Research. The past.	What does the past have to tell me?
Light	Illumination. Vision.	What am I ready to see?
Lighthouse	Self-illumination. Warning. Guidance.	What do I need to see to avoid danger?
Lightning	Flash of illumination. Sudden vision.	What is awakening in me?
Limousine See also **Vehicles**.	Luxurious power. Extravagance.	Where in my life am I ready to be conspicuous in my expression of power?
Limping	Work on freedom of movement. One-sidedness.	What balance am I seeking? Which side am I developing?
Lion See also **Animals, wild**.	Nobility. Strength. Pride.	Where does courage dwell in me?
Lips	Invitation. Communication.	What am I offering or what is offered to me?
Lipstick	Enhancement. Attraction. Confidence.	What do I feature?
Little	Smaller than usual. Reduced. Insignificant.	Where in my life do I feel diminished? What am I ready to reduce?

Image	Associations	Ask Yourself
Lively	High energy. Vitality.	What activates me?
Liver	Bad feelings. Sluggishness.	What peace am I seeking? In what way am I ready to be compassionate?
Living room See also **House.**	Central space of the house of self.	What is central to my being?
Lizard See also **Animals, wild.**	Cold-blooded. Reptilian.	Where in my life am I ready to show more warmth?
Load	Encumbrance. Burden.	What am I ready to put down? Where in my life do I want to lighten up?
Lobby	Public space.	What am I willing to make known?
Lock	Security. Confinement.	What am I ready to open up or close away?
Locker See also **School.**	Storage. Safekeeping.	What have I stored away? What am I ready to remember?
Looking	Consideration. Attention.	What do I pay attention to?
Lost	Without direction. Missing.	Where in my life am I lacking in confidence?

Image	Associations	Ask Yourself
Lottery See also **Gambling.**	Chance. Good fortune. Risk.	Where in my life do I look for a large benefit at little cost?
Love/Loving	Unconditional acceptance.	Where do I feel complete?
Lover	The idealized inner self. Anima. Animus.	What part of my larger self is ready to be integrated?
Low See also **Down.**	Accessible. Inferior.	What is down there?
Luggage See also **Baggage.**	Belongings. Beliefs.	What am I taking with me? What am I ready to leave behind?
Lumber See also **Wood.**	Supplies for growth.	What am I building or constructing?
Lungs See also **Body parts.**	Breath of life. Freedom.	In what ways is my life ready to expand?
Lust See also **Sex.**	Eagerness for possession.	What will satisfy me? Where in my life am I unfulfilled?
Machine	Automatic. Efficiency. Unthinking.	What feelings am I ignoring? What drudgery am I ready to give up?
Maestro	Mastery.	What abilities am I ready to claim?

Image	Associations	Ask Yourself
Magazine	Stimulation. Consumption.	Where in my life are my desires unrealized?
Mage See also **Magician**.	Work on physical and spiritual worlds.	What do I seek to integrate?
Magician	Work on command of inner and outer worlds or forces. Transformation.	What powers do I control or fear?
Mail	News. Guidance.	What do I want to hear or learn?
Mail carrier	Work on communication.	What do I want to hear or say?
Makeup	Image. Feminine projection.	Who do I show to the world?
Male	Yang aspect of self. Assertion.	What action am I ready to take?
Mall	Central resources. Community. Consumption.	What needs or desires do I share with others?
Man	Yang aspect. Active.	Where in my life am I ready to be more assertive?
Manager	Work on organization.	How am I ready to be more efficient?

Image	Associations	Ask Yourself
Mandala	The totality of the self. Wholeness.	Where in my life am I ready to express my totality of being?
Mansion See also **House.**	Expansive residence of the self.	What part of me needs more room?
Map	Guidance. Directions.	What information do I need to make my journey?
Marble	Ornamental purity. Endurance.	What do I value for its beauty and strength?
Marriage	Union. Commitment.	What am I ready to join or commit myself to?
Martial arts	Disciplined strength or force.	How am I refining my power?
Mask	Disguise. Persona. Attitudes.	What do I hide? What do I display?
Masturbation See also **Sex.**	Self-love.	What part of myself am I ready to accept and love?
Matador See also **Bullfight.**	Work on bravery.	What challenge am I preparing to face?
Matches	Ignition. Minor illumination.	What do I want to kindle?

Image	Associations	Ask Yourself
Maze	Puzzle. Labyrinth.	What intricate problems am I ready to solve?
Meat	Essential nourishment. Sometimes a need to survive.	What must I do to survive? Where am I ready to trust?
Mechanic	Repair. Make good. Work on what has been damaged.	What damage am I ready to restore?
Medicine	Healing. Antidote.	Where in my life am I ready to be healthy and whole?
Melting See also **Water**.	Letting go.	What old structures am I ready to dissolve?
Memory	Past. Record.	What old self is ready for transformation?
Menstruation	Power or fear of feminine identity.	Where am I ready to express more natural power?
Mentally deficient	Innocence. Lack of development.	What must I care for in myself?
Mercury	Liveliness. Inconstancy.	What part of me seeks stability? Where in my life do I feel stuck?

Image	Associations	Ask Yourself
Mermaid/Merman	Emotional part of identity.	What do I want to feel?
Merry-go-round	Innocent fun. Mindless repetition.	What simple pleasures satisfy me? Do I feel trapped by circumstances?
Messy	Disorder.	What do I want to clear up?
Metal	Endurance. Rigidity. Resolution.	Where in my life must I stand firm?
Microphone	Communication.	Where in my life am I ready to speak out?
Microwave	Accelerated processing.	What am I in a hurry for?
Middle	Halfway between.	Which way do I want to go?
Midget See also **Dwarf.**	Work on insufficiency.	What wants to be larger in me?
Mildew	Emotional rot.	What feelings are ready to be brought to light?
Military	Work on aggression.	Where in my life am I threatened? What strengthens me?
Milk See also **Food.**	Maternal love. Sustenance. Kindness.	What part of me is developing and seeks nourishment

Image	Associations	Ask Yourself
Mine	Hidden riches. The unconscious.	What treasures are buried deep within me?
Minister	Work on compassion or care giving.	Where in my life am I ready to be more understanding?
Minotaur	Union of beastly and human nature.	Where in my life is blind impulse a threat to me?
Miracle	Supernatural wonder.	Where in my life do I feel the perfection of my own being?
Mirror	Image. Identity.	What part of me is reflected? What am I ready to see?
Miserable	Loss. Fear of deprivation.	What do I need to have to be happy?
Mist See also Water.	Delicate expanse of feeling. Cool and comfortable.	What emotional field surrounds me?
Mistake	Self-doubt.	What am I ready to accept in myself?
Mistletoe See also Kissing.	Flirtation. Attraction.	What or whom do I wish to attract?

Image	Associations	Ask Yourself
Mix	Uniting. Confusion.	What is coming together, for better or worse?
Mob See also **Crowd.**	Loss of organizing principle or control.	Where in my life am I ready to command my conflicting desires?
Modern	Present. Up to date.	What am I leaving behind?
Moment	Immediacy.	What is important?
Monastery	Spiritual community. Withdrawal from worldly affairs.	Where in my life do I seek to join with my spiritual peers?
Money	Security. Riches.	What do I value?
Monk	Retreat. Spiritual life.	What part of me needs to withdraw from life's demands?
Monkey See also **Animals, wild.**	Dexterity. Mischief. Humor.	What part of me is almost human?
Monster	Denied self. Threat.	What do I fear in myself?
Monument	Work on worthiness or recognition.	What do I value in myself? How do I wish to be remembered?

Image	Associations	Ask Yourself
Moon	Emotion. Reflection. Inner self.	What feelings do I reflect?
Mosquito	Minor annoyance.	What irritates me?
Mosquito net	Defense from annoyance.	What am I protected against?
Moss	Stillness. Slow growth.	Where in my life am I ready to be more patient?
Mother	Nurturance. Approval or disapproval.	What do I care for in myself?
Motorcycle See also **Vehicles.**	Virility. Vigor. Display.	How hot am I? Where in my life am I ready to be more masterful?
Mountain	Aspiration. Success through effort.	What am I ready to achieve?
Mouse See also **Animals, wild.**	Meek nature. Quiet. Minor problems. Inner feelings. Shyness.	What small troubles are gnawing away at me?
Mouth See also **Body parts.**	Nourishment. New attitudes.	What am I ready to take in? What am I ready to express?
Movie star	Glamour. Recognition. Fame.	What part of me is ready to be in the spotlight?

Image	Associations	Ask Yourself
Moving	New life. A fresh start.	What lies ahead for me? What am I ready to leave behind?
Mud See also **Water.**	Messy feelings. Fertility. Stuck.	What emotions am I ready to clean up? What is growing?
Mule See also **Animals, domestic.**	Obstinate. Intractable. Stamina.	Where in my life am I ready to persevere?
Mummy	Reverence for the past. Ancient wisdom.	What do I wish to preserve or remember? What endures in me?
Murder	Violent completion.	What will I do anything to end?
Muscles See also **Body parts.**	Power. Strength.	What power am I ready to develop?
Museum	Past merit. Culture.	What am I ready to learn from?
Music	Harmony. Expression.	What am I integrating?
Musician See also **Music; Dancing.**	Work on harmony or creativity.	What inspires me?
Mute	Speechless.	What am I afraid to say? Or what do I wish to say?

Image	Associations	Ask Yourself
Myth	Real or imagined past.	What story do I want to change?
Naked	Exposed. Vulnerable.	Where am I ready to be seen?
Nap *See also* **Dreaming; Sleeping.**	Relaxation and rest. Ease.	What part of me needs to take it easy?
Narrow	Restriction. Tight.	Where do I seek more room?
Native	Intuitive self. Harmony with nature. Primordial being.	Where in my life do I seek alignment with nature?
Native American	Stoicism. Natural wisdom. Cunning.	What is untamed in me? Where in my life do I want more freedom from control?
Nativity	Peace. Birth of spirit.	What revelation am I seeking?
Nature	Wholeness of being.	Where do I feel incomplete?
Navy	Command of feeling. Sometimes homosexual undertones.	What emotions am I ready to command?
Nazi	Totalitarian control. Sentimentality.	What extreme reactions am I ready to adjust?

Image	Associations	Ask Yourself
Neat	In good order.	What do I want to clear up?
Neck *See also* **Body parts.**	Flexibility, especially of vision.	What can I see if I make a small adjustment?
Necking *See also* **Sex.**	Seduction. Intimacy.	What intimacy am I ready for?
Necklace *See also* **Jewelry.**	Display. Distinction.	What am I proud of? What do I value in myself?
Needle	Piercing.	Where in my life am I ready to get the point? What do I wish penetrate?
Neighbor	Fellowship.	What is close to me? What do I like or fear about myself?
Neighborhood	Work on community.	Where in my life am I ready to join with others?
Nerd	Insignificant but smart. Absence of charm.	Where in my life am I ready to be as attractive as I am smart?
Nervous	Insecurity. Self-doubt.	Where am I becoming more self-assured?

Image	Associations	Ask Yourself
Nest	Safety. Comfort.	Where in my life do I seek protection? What comforts me?
Nets	Safety. Entrapment.	Where in my life am I ready to be fearless?
New	Unused. Novel.	What bores me? Where do I want stimulation?
Newspaper	Ephemeral data.	What is changing every moment?
Night	Mystery. Unconscious contents. Inner vision.	What darkness am I ready to penetrate?
Nightclub See also **Night.**	Stimulation. Entertainment.	What excitement do I seek?
Nine See also **Numbers.**	Hidden blessings. Completion. Compassion.	What is revealed to me?
Nobility	Excellence or false elevation.	What do I aspire to or judge as false?
Noise	Chaos. Confusion.	What distracts me?
Normal	Effortless control.	What comfort do I draw from familiarity?
North	Death and transformation. End of the journey.	What do I want to end whatever the cost?

Image	Associations	Ask Yourself
North Pole	Point of transformation. End of the journey.	What is over or complete for me?
Nose *See also* **Body parts.**	Instinctive knowledge.	How does it smell to me? What do I know without knowing?
Nuclear waste	Shadow side of progress.	What advance endangers me?
Numbers *See also* **subheadings.**	We lack a consistent cultural tradition for the interpretation of numbers. If a number appears repeatedly in a dream, or if it is highlighted, first ask yourself what personal significance it has for you. It may refer to an important date in your life, to a well-remembered address or birth date, or to other events or experiences. Begin by identifying these personal associations. Below is a common interpretation of numbers one through ten, with the addition of numbers eleven, twenty-two, and thirty-three. Dream consciousness is always hungry for new material; this system can easily be digested if you find it nourishing.	
— one	Beginning. Oneness. Essence. Individual will.	Who am I?
— two	Duality. Opposition. Balance. Partnership.	How do I relate?
— three	Trinity. Balance of opposites. Sociability.	How do I integrate my differences?

Image	Associations	Ask Yourself
— *four*	Stability. Matter. Potential for sudden change. Worldly effort.	Where in my life am I most stable?
— *five*	Quintessence. Change. Celebration.	What is evolving in me?
— *six*	Expansion. Organization. Harmony. Domesticity.	What am I ready to commit to?
— *seven*	Energy given form. Cycles of growth. Discipline.	What am I ready to learn?
— *eight*	Eternity. Abundance. Power. Cosmic consciousness.	What am I willing to receive?
— *nine*	Hidden blessings. Completion. Compassion.	What is revealed to me?
— *ten*	New beginning on a higher octave.	What have I learned?
— *eleven*	Inspiration. Revolution. Higher octave of two.	What am I ready to change?
— *twenty-two*	Earthly mission. Self and others.	What do I trust?
— *thirty-three*	Salvation and temptation.	Where in my life have I succeeded or failed?

Image	Associations	Ask Yourself
Nun	Spiritual dedication.	What worldly demands weary me?
Nurse	Healing care. Compassion.	What part of me needs to be cared for or needs to care for others?
Nut	Essence. Kernel. Richness.	What is essential to my nourishment?
Nylon	Carefree. Unnatural.	Where do I want to be untroubled?
Oasis	Place of refuge and relaxation.	Where in my life do I seek a sanctuary?
Ocean *See also* **Water.**	Vast, limitless feeling. Sometimes an overwhelming emotion. Rich with abundant life.	What part of me relates to such vastness?
Octopus	Shy. Grasping.	What do I need to hold onto?
Office	Workplace. Professional aspect of self.	What am I working on or with?
Oil	Lubricity. Slipperiness.	What do I want to get unstuck? Where do I seek more freedom of movement?

Image	Associations	Ask Yourself
Oily	Smarminess. Fawning.	Where in my life am I ready to be more direct?
Old	Maturity. Degeneration.	What is complete for me? What am I ready to replace?
One See also **Numbers.**	Beginning. Oneness. Essence. Individual will.	Who am I?
Open	Opportunity. Potential.	What choice am I ready to make?
Opera	Elaborate or complex form. Epic.	What grandeur do I seek in my life?
Opossum See also **Animals, wild.**	Feigning death.	What threatens me? Where am I ready to come to life?
Oracle	Prophecy. Ambiguity. Riddle.	What is becoming clear to me? What can I successfully decipher?
Oral sex See also **Sex.**	Gratification. Pleasure.	What part of me wants to give or receive gratification?
Orange See also **Colors.**	Emotion. Stimulation. Healing.	What am I feeling?
Orchard	Fruitful growth.	What are the results of my productivity?

Image	Associations	Ask Yourself
Orchid	Exotic glamour.	What is uniquely beautiful in me? How am I different from others?
Order	Habit. Control.	What must I get together?
Organizing	Work on belief or confidence.	What am I ready to trust?
Orgasm See also **Sex**.	Consummation.	What is complete for me?
Orgy See also **Sex**.	Indiscriminate union.	Where in my life am I ready to experience the oneness of all?
Oriental See also **East**.	Eastern wisdom. Subtlety.	Where in my life is wisdom developing for me?
Orphan	Lack of protection. Isolation.	What deep connections am I preparing to make?
Ostrich	Denial. Grounded.	What am I ready to deal with? What freedom do I seek?
Outer space See also **Rocket**; **Spaceship**.	Transcendence of personal reality.	What larger being do I seek to experience?

Image	Associations	Ask Yourself
Outlaw	Rebellion. Adventure.	What freedom do I seek?
Outside See also **Nature.**	What is conscious. Outer part.	What do I show to the world?
Overalls See also **Clothing.**	Common. Sturdiness. Protection.	What do I cover? What work is hard for me?
Owl	Wisdom. Vision.	What part of me is naturally wise?
Ox See also **Animals, domestic.**	Burden. Strength. Stupidity.	How do I doubt my own strength? What makes me feel stupid?
Oyster See also **Food.**	Tender inside, hard outside. Sexual stimulation.	What am I hungry for?
Pack	Load. Burden. Equipment.	What do I carry with me?
Package	Expectation. Mystery.	What am I looking for? What do I fear to find?
Packing	Preparation for movement. Sorting or storing old ideas.	What do I want to take or leave behind?
Pager	Accessibility. Availability.	What part of me is always on call?

Image	Associations	Ask Yourself
Pain	Conflict. Problem. Suffering.	What hurts me? What parts of my self are denied?
Painting See also **Art; Artist.**	Transforming. Decorating.	What do I wish to change or improve?
Palace See also **House.**	Potential kingdom of the self.	How can I fulfill my potential?
Pan See also **Satyr.**	Divinity of nature. Unleashing.	What elemental aspects of my nature am I coming to terms with?
Pan (cooking utensil)	Basic equipment. Utensil.	What am I ready to prepare?
Panther See also **Animals, wild.**	Wild beauty. Grace.	What force do I wish or fear to unleash?
Panties See also **Clothing.**	Private self. Sexual identity.	What are my hidden feelings? What am I ready to expose?
Parachute	Rescue. Deliverance.	What am I escaping from? Where do I want to land?
Parade	Fanciful display. Options.	What part of me wants to be seen?
Paralysis	Resistance. No change or growth.	What move am I preparing to make?

Image	Associations	Ask Yourself
Paranoia	Work on obsessive fear.	What inner strength am I ready to recognize?
Parasite	Work on independence.	Where am I ready to fend for myself?
Paratrooper	Invasion. The thrill of physical danger.	What territory do I want to encounter?
Parents See also **Father; Mother.**	Authority. Source.	What decisions do I wish or fear to make?
Park See also **Nature.**	Control of nature.	Where would I like or fear to run wild?
Parking lot See also **Vehicles.**	Potential power and movement.	What power waits for me to take off?
Parrot	Imitative. Humorous. Exotic.	Where in my life do I lack originality?
Partner	Affiliation. Mutual goals.	What do I need for fulfillment?
Party	Celebration. Festivity.	What am I ready to celebrate?
Passport	Freedom of movement. Identity.	What part of me wants to expand and explore?
Past	Memory	What lies behind me?

Image	Associations	Ask Yourself
Pastry See also **Cake**.	Luxury. Indulgence. Sweetness.	What do I crave? Is there enough sweetness in my life?
Path	Life's direction.	What do I feel about my chosen route?
Patience	Self-regard. Faith.	What do I trust in?
Pattern	Established order.	What beliefs am I examining?
Paw See also **Animals, domestic; Animals, wild**.	Handling animal instincts.	Where in my life am I ready to trust my intuition?
Peace	Inner harmony.	What have I resolved within myself?
Peacock	Pride and vanity. Display.	What do I wish to have seen or admired?
Peak See also **Mountain**.	Point of success. Achievement.	What am I heading for?
Pearl See also **Jewel**.	Purity. Treasure. Transforming irritation to beauty.	What do I value? How is it created?
Pebbles	Serenity. Compactness.	What is coming together for me? What edges have been smoothed away?

Image	Associations	Ask Yourself
Pedestal	Support. Inflation. Display. Admiration.	What do I wish or fear to show off? What do I look up to?
Peek/Peeking	Secrets. Curiosity.	What will I risk for information?
Penis See also **Body parts.**	Male sexuality. Yang power.	How is my power expressed?
Performing	Accomplishment. Achievement.	Where in my life do I seek recognition?
Perfume	Luxury. Indulgence. Balm.	What gratifies me? Where in my life do I seek more pleasure?
Pet See also **Animals, domestic.**	Work on self-love.	What part of myself do I care for?
Petticoat See also **Clothing: slip.**	Modesty. Inner feminine.	What am I ready or hesitant to reveal?
Pharaoh	Absolute authority. Union of human with divinity.	What form of authority do I fear or trust in myself?
Philanthropist	Generosity of spirit.	What riches am I prepared to share?
Phoenix	Rebirth. Renewal. Immortality.	What part of me cannot die?

Image	Associations	Ask Yourself
Photograph	Image. Vision. Memory.	What do I remember? How do I see the world?
Photographer **See also** Camera.	Work on world image.	What image of the world do I want to preserve?
Picnic	Lighthearted nourishment.	Where in my life am I ready to be more carefree?
Pig **See also** Animals, domestic.	Greedy. Smart. Sometimes slovenly, sometimes fastidious.	Am I grabbing more than I need or can use? Do I clean up my own mess?
Pigeon **See also** Bird.	Victimhood.	Where in my life am I ready to stand up for myself?
Pill	Aid. Relief. Medicine.	What do I need to feel better?
Pillow	Comfort. Intimacy.	What part of me seeks encouragement?
Pilot	Work on freedom of movement and change.	What destination am I hurrying toward?
Pimples	Ugliness. Small bursts of anger.	How am I ready to be less sensitive?

Image	Associations	Ask Yourself
Pink *See also* **Colors.**	Affection. Love.	To what am I responding?
Pins	Minor corrections.	What am I joining together?
Pirate	Outlaw. Rejection of social rules and obligations.	What rules do I reject? Where do I feel restricted by society?
Pizza	Indulgence. Informality.	Where do I want to relax?
Plague	Universal disorder or disease.	What system do I believe is breaking down?
Plane *See also* **Vehicles.**	Rapid movement across great distance.	Am I in a hurry for change?
Planets	Cosmic harmony and influence. Celestial order.	Am I in or out of harmony with heavenly power?
Plants	Nature. Natural process. Fertility.	What is growing in me?
Plastic	Artificiality. Cheap substitute. Resilience.	What is the real thing?
Platform	Position. Stage.	What do I want to present?

Image	Associations	Ask Yourself
Play	Performance. Script or production of life.	What changes in my life script am I considering?
Playing	Carefreeness. Joy.	Where in my life do I want more fun?
Playsuit See also **Clothing**.	Child aspect of self.	Where in my life do I want more enjoyment?
Plumber/Plumbing	Work on emotional release.	What part of me needs clearing out or replacing?
Poetry	Quintessence of meaning.	What is essential for me?
Poison	Destructive actions or thoughts.	What no longer nourishes me?
Poker	Strategy. Finesse.	What game do I play?
Police	Work on order or control.	Where in my life do I seek order or fear control?
Politician	Work on policy. Choosing sides. Manipulation.	What side am I on? Where do I want to win?
Polyester	Cheap substitute. Convenience.	Where am I making do?

Image	Associations	Ask Yourself
Pond See also **Water.**	Contained feelings. Tranquility.	What emotions do I hold close?
Poor	Self-judgment. Insecurity.	What inner riches am I ready to claim?
Popcorn	Lively pleasure.	What is fun for me?
Porch See also **House.**	Intersection of self with the world.	Where in my life am I ready to be more approachable?
Pornography See also **Sex.**	Work on intimacy. Anonymous sex.	What part of myself am I afraid of exposing?
Power	Resources. Self-trust.	How is self-sufficiency expanding within me?
Praying	Communion. Seeking help.	Where in my life am I ready to surrender?
Pregnancy	New life. Fecundity.	What am I preparing to produce?
Premature ejaculation See also **Sex.**	Bad timing. Loss of control.	What feelings overwhelm me?
President	Leadership or lack of leadership.	Where in my life am I ready or reluctant to lead?
Pretty	Attraction.	What appeals to me?

Image	Associations	Ask Yourself
Priest	Work on spiritual or religious well-being. Release.	What am I ready to forgive?
Primitive	Basic instincts.	Am I overcivilized? Where do I want to be more natural?
Prince	Noble aspect of self. Refined masculinity.	What do I admire or seek in men or in myself?
Princess	Noble aspect of self. Refined femininity.	What do I admire to seek in women or in myself?
Prison	Punishment. Confinement.	Where have I done wrong?
Prize	Accomplishment. Rewards.	What do I deserve or long for?
Procession See also **Parade.**	Ceremonial march. Pomp.	What beliefs am I ready to formalize or observe?
Project	Goal. Purpose.	What am I ready to accomplish?
Property	Substance. Responsibility.	What do I own or wish to own?
Prostitute	If negative, misuse of sexuality. If positive, sexual healing.	What do I need to feel sexually healthy?

Image	Associations	Ask Yourself
Pruning	Elimination of old growth.	What old stuff am I ready to cut away?
Psychic	Work on intuition, expanded consciousness.	In what way do I seek limitless awareness?
Psychokinesis	Power of consciousness over matter.	In what ways am I ready to take control of the world?
Pubic hair	Modesty. Sexual display.	What sexual feelings do I conceal or expose?
Puddle **See also** Water.	Small but messy emotions.	What minor discomfort am I feeling?
Pulley	Movement with minimal effort.	What is easy for me to shift?
Punks	Alienation. Protest.	What part of me wants more love and attention?
Puppet	Fear of control. Weak will.	Where am I ready to assert myself?
Pure	Innocence. Virtue.	What do I forgive in myself or others?
Purse **See also** Clothing.	Feminine self. Sometimes sexual identity. Security.	What am I holding onto? What part of myself do I value?

Image	Associations	Ask Yourself
Pursuit	Denied power.	What part of myself frightens me? Where can my strength be expressed safely?
Pyramid	Communication with greater consciousness. Ancient knowledge.	What height of awareness am I seeking?
Python See also **Snake**.	Overpowering energy.	What crushes and consumes me?
Queen	Noble aspect of femininity.	Where in my life am I ready to express feminine power?
Quest See also **Searching**.	Adventure. Soul seeking.	What part of me holds the answer?
Quicksand	Insecurity. Instability.	Where in my life do I want a stronger foundation?
Quiet	Absence of information. Peace.	What have I completed?
Rabbit See also **Animals, domestic; Animals, wild.**	Fertility. Luck. Insecurity.	Where in my life am I ready to be productive?
Raccoon See also **Animals, wild.**	Cleverness. Ingenuity.	What trouble am I getting into?

Image	Associations	Ask Yourself
Race	Contest. Rivalry.	What is my goal? What am I missing by being in a hurry?
Radio	Story about reality. Communication.	What am I ready to hear or say?
Rafters See also **House.**	Protective support.	What supports my higher consciousness?
Rage	Work on victimhood.	What inner strength am I searching for?
Rain See also **Water.**	Release of emotion. May be gentle and nourishing or dramatically threatening.	What feelings are pouring down on me?
Rainbow	Promise. Visible blessing.	What encourages me? Where do I expect to find happiness?
Rape See also **Sex.**	Forced union.	What do I fear being forced to unite with?
Rapids See also **Water.**	Active, stimulating emotions.	How comfortable am I with intense feelings?
Rapist See also **Sex.**	Forcing union.	Where in my life do I feel my love is rejected?
Rash	Irritations. Incidental anger.	How does caution restrict me? Am I too impetuous?

Image	Associations	Ask Yourself
Rat See also **Animals, wild.**	Street smarts. Clever. Sneaky and untrustworthy.	Where in my life do I fear betrayal? Can I trust myself?
Rattlesnake See also **Poison; Snake.**	Poisonous energy.	What warning am I hearing?
Raven	Magic. Omen. Sagacity.	What is the source of my wisdom?
Razor	Keen. Sharpness. Edge.	What do I want to cut off or make smooth?
Reading See also **Book; Bookstore.**	Exploring alternate realities or escape from present.	What worlds lie within me? What burdens me?
Recipe	Formula. Pattern.	What am I learning to do or make?
Red See also **Colors.**	Energy. Vigor. Passion.	What is my source of energy or strength?
Redhead See also **Blond; Brunette.**	Tempestuous. Dramatic. Spontaneous.	Where in my life do I want more vitality?
Reef See also **Water.**	Danger or safety of hidden emotions.	What underlies my feelings?
Reflection See also **Mirror.**	Self-image.	What am I ready to see or to understand?
Refrigerator	Chilling to preserve.	What do I want to save?

Image	Associations	Ask Yourself
Rehabilitation	A fresh start.	What part of myself am I ready to rebuild?
Rehearsal	Practice.	What skills do I want to perfect?
Relatives See also **Family.**	Unrecognized aspects of self.	What parts of my being am I ready to acknowledge?
Remodeling See also **House.**	Restructuring the house of self.	What part of me needs more room or renewal? How do I want to appear to the world?
Repairing	Work on what has been damaged.	What am I ready to fix?
Restaurant	Place of nourishment. Choices.	What do I want to order?
Retarded See also **Mentally deficient.**	Work on development and training or education.	Where in my life do I want to catch up with others? Where do I fear being behind?
Reunion	Meeting with unrecognized aspects of self.	What part of my past am I ready to remember?
Rhinestone	Imitation. Cheap substitute.	Where in my life am I ready for the real thing?

Image	Associations	Ask Yourself
Rhinoceros See also **Animals, wild.**	Blind strength. Armoring.	What am I ready to see or understand about my power?
Rich/Riches	Worth. Security.	What do I wish or fear to possess?
Right	The mind. Action.	What is it time for me to do?
Ring	Pledge. Commitment. Promise.	What union do I seek?
Riot See also **Mob.**	Loss of individuality. Destructive conformity.	Where in my life am I ready to stand alone?
Ritual	Energy created through repetition.	What tradition sustains me?
River See also **Water.**	Flowing and active. May include dangerous rapids; may be smooth and tranquil.	What feelings are actively moving within me?
Road	Direction. Life's path.	Where am I going?
Roadblock	Barrier to fulfillment.	What blocks my path?
Robot	Mechanical aspect of self.	What freedom do I seek?
Rock See also **Stone.**	Immutability. Security.	What do I want to make permanent?

Image	Associations	Ask Yourself
Rocket *See also* **Outer space; Spaceship.**	Breaking free of physical limits. Exploration of inner space.	What limitations am I ready to transcend?
Rocking	Comfort. Grief.	What solace or relief am I seeking?
Rodeo	Exhibition of skill. Human control of animal force.	Where am I ready to display my skill at mastering wild forces?
Rollerblades	Rapid movement with ease. Thrills.	What new freedom excites me?
Roller coaster	Ups and downs. Thrills and chills. Wild but safe ride.	What excitement do I crave? How can I better enjoy the ride?
Roof *See also* **House.**	Above. Protection. Covering.	Where in my life am I ready to expand my limitations?
Rooster	Aggressive masculinity. Conceit.	What do I want to crow about?
Roots	Grounding. Nourishment.	What connects me to my source?
Rope	Connecting. Restraint.	What do I wish to join together or to control?
Rosary	Devotion. Piety.	What do I worship?

Image	Associations	Ask Yourself
Rose	Goodness. Wholeness. Integration.	What is coming together within me?
Rotten	Wasted potential.	What have I failed to make use of?
Rough	Difficult. Undeveloped.	Where do I seek a smoother way?
Ruby See also **Jewel.**	Passionate awareness. Intensity. Sacred blood.	What do I care deeply about?
Running	Rapid movement. Escape. Joy of the physical. Impatience.	What moves me? What am I after?
Rusty	Deterioration.	Where do I feel unprotected?
R.V. See also **Vehicles.**	The joy of power. Rugged amusement.	Where in my life am I ready to enjoy the expression of power?
Sad See also **Sorrow.**	Work on disappointment.	What will make me happy?
Sadomasochism See also **Sex.**	Control of passion or instinct.	How does pain make me feel in control?
Safari	Freedom from civilization.	What confinements am I ready to be free from?
Safe	Trust. Inner strength.	What fears have I mastered?

Image	Associations	Ask Yourself
Safety pins	Holding together.	What needs to be joined for safekeeping?
Sage	Work on wisdom or understanding.	Where in my life do I want to apply thought and good judgment?
Sailor See also **Navy.**	Navigating emotional seas.	What feelings am I taking charge of?
Sale See also **Prize.**	A bargain. Opportunity.	What can I readily access? What do I fear is out of my reach?
Salesperson See also **Shopping.**	Service. Availability.	What do I want to include in my life?
Salmon	Indomitability.	What powerful feelings can I depend on?
Salt	Savor. Flavor. Intensification.	What do I want to enhance in my life?
Samurai	Work on allegiance. Honor.	What am I committed to? Do my obligations limit me?
Sand	Barrenness. Immeasurability.	What is eternal in me? What prevents my growth?
Sandbox	Playful construction.	What new forms am I taking too seriously?

Image	Associations	Ask Yourself
Sandpaper	Abrasiveness.	What roughness do I want to rub away?
Santa Claus	Belief. Getting what you want.	What do I believe I want?
Satellite	Message. Expansion through technology.	What distant news am I ready to hear?
Satyr See also **Goat; Man.**	Work on union of intellect with animal passion.	Where in my life am I integrating my mind and my body? Where do I seek sexual freedom?
Saw	Severing. Separation.	What am I forming?
Scar	Healed wound. Incomplete release of emotional hurt.	What am I ready to heal completely?
School	Education. Discipline.	What do I need to learn? What have I already learned and no longer need to study?
Scientist	Work on understanding or knowledge.	What do I want to comprehend or describe?
Scissors	Feminine weapon. Separation.	What do I wish to cut out?
Scooter See also **Vehicles.**	Playful expression of power?	How am I enjoying the ride?

Image	Associations	Ask Yourself
Scorpion	Destructive feelings, thoughts, words.	Where in my life am I ready to express my authority and power?
Screw	Strong connection.	What am I joining together?
Screwdriver	Work on connection.	What am I preparing to connect?
Scum	Worthless debris.	What self-judgment am I discarding?
Seal See also **Animals, wild.**	Comic instinct. Playfulness.	Where do I seek more joy in life?
Search engine	Boundaryless exploration.	What new worlds attract me?
Searching See also **Quest.**	Recognition of desire or wants. Acknowledgment of need.	What am I finally ready to find?
Seasick	Sickening emotions.	What feelings am I ready to get rid of?
Seat belt See also **Vehicles.**	Safety. Restraint.	What holds my power in check?
Seaweed	Growth within emotion. Can be nourishing or strangling.	What is developing in my sea of feeling?

Image	Associations	Ask Yourself
Secondhand	Cheap. Serviceable.	Where in my life am I willing to make do or what am I willing to be satisfied by?
Secret	Work on what is hidden.	What am I ready to expose or uncover?
Secretary	Organization. Order. Help.	Where in my life do I need to get organized?
Security guard	Work on safety.	What part of me needs protection?
Security system	Safety insurance.	What defenses am I preparing to dismantle?
Sedative	Forgetfulness. Escape.	What is too stimulating or demanding for me?
Seed	Beginning. Source of greater being.	What or where do I wish to develop?
Seizures	Extreme agitation. Spasmodic movement.	Where in my life do I fear or seek control?
Self-defense	Work on anger.	What inner strength do I seek?
Self-immolation	Burning pain.	What must I destroy in order to feel alive?
Semen See also Sex.	Yang aspect of fertility. Potency.	What am I bringing into being?

Image	Associations	Ask Yourself
Senile	Work on declining abilities.	What is no longer important to me?
Seven *See also* **Numbers.**	Energy given form. Cycles of growth. Discipline.	What am I ready to learn?
Sewer	Accumulation of negativity. Release.	What junk am I ready to get rid of?
Sewing	Joining together. Repair.	What do I want to create or restore?
Sex *See subheadings.*		
— affair	Surrender. Ardor.	What do I wish to yield to?
— anal	Submission. Union without issue.	To what or to whom do I want or fear to yield?
— arousal	Stimulation. Availability.	What do I want to respond to?
— bestiality	Union with animal passions or instincts.	What basic aspects of myself do I fear or deny?
— erection	Creative power. Fertility.	What do I want to do or to make?
— exhibitionism	Exposure.	What part of myself do I need to see or to understand?

Image	Associations	Ask Yourself
— *extramarital*	Illicit union.	What is lacking in my relationship with myself?
— *homosexual*	Union — or fear of union — with aspects of self.	What part of my femininity or masculinity do I seek to merge with?
— *hugging*	Loving protection. Acknowledgment.	What part of me needs more attention?
— *incest*	Fear of love.	Am I ready to be sexually mature?
— *intercourse*	Union. Release. Pleasure. Creation.	What do I want or fear to merge with?
— *kissing*	Intimacy. Affection. Greeting.	What or whom do I wish to be close to?
— *lust*	Eagerness for possession.	What will satisfy me? Where in my life am I unfulfilled?
— *masturbation*	Self-love.	What part of myself am I ready to love and accept?
— *oral*	Gratification. Pleasure.	What part of me wants to give or receive gratification?
— *orgasm*	Consummation.	What is complete for me?

Image	Associations	Ask Yourself
— *orgy*	Indiscriminate union.	Where in my life am I ready to experience the oneness of all?
— *pornography*	Work on intimacy. Anonymous sex.	What part of myself am I afraid of exposing?
— *premature ejaculation*	Bad timing. Loss of control.	What feelings overwhelm me?
— *rape*	Forced union.	What do I fear being forced to unite with?
— *rapist*	Forcing union.	Where in my life do I feel my love is rejected?
— *sadomasochism*	Control of passion or instinct.	How does pain make me feel in control?
— *semen*	Yang aspect of fertility. Potency.	What am I bringing into being?
— *voyeurism*	Safe distant from desires.	What do I want or fear to be close to?
Shack See also **House.**	Undeveloped self.	Where am I ready to remodel and expand?
Shadow	Hidden. Dark side of image.	What am I ready to illuminate?
Shaman	Manipulation of reality.	What part of my world am I transforming?

Image	Associations	Ask Yourself
Shame	Work on self-respect.	What do I value in myself?
Shark	Dangers lurking in emotion.	What powerful feeling is threatening me?
Shaving *See also* **Beard; Leg.**	Self-maintenance, sometimes onerous. Keeping up appearances.	Where do I feel conflict or pride in my self-image?
Shed	Storage of ideas or skills.	What am I saving or holding onto?
Sheep *See also* **Animals, domestic.**	Conformity.	What am I following?
Shell	Protection. Can be limiting or covering. Beauty of form.	Which feelings do I need to protect? What structures do I value?
Shield	Protection. Security. Defense.	Where in my life am I ready to be more vulnerable?
Shining	High energy. Beacon.	How do I wish to be seen? What attracts me?
Shirt *See also* **Clothing.**	Upper, as opposed to lower, self. Emotions.	What feelings do I consider appropriate?

Image	Associations	Ask Yourself
Shock	Sudden awakening. Illumination.	What arouses me? What awareness electrifies me?
Shoes See also **Clothing.**	General situation. Grounding.	How well do I connect with the world?
Shooting	Destroying aspects of self.	What do I want to get rid of?
Shopping	Finding what you want. Options.	What am I ready to take home?
Shorts See also **Clothing.**	Private self. Sexual identity.	What are my hidden feelings? What am I ready to expose?
Shotgun See also **Gun.**	Widespread violence.	What damage is spreading around me?
Shoulders See also **Body parts.**	Strength or burdens.	What am I ready to carry? What is too heavy for me?
Shovel	Unearthing. Planting.	What am I digging up?
Shower	Cleansing. Release down the drain.	What do I want to wash away?
Shrimp	Insignificant. Of small value.	Where in my life am I ready to feel more worthy?

Image	Associations	Ask Yourself
Shrine *See also* Temple.	Sacred part of self.	What part of me is worthy? What do I worship in myself?
Shrinking	Inadequacy. Too small.	Where in my life — or by whom — do I feel diminished?
Shy	Work on self-confidence.	What do I trust in myself?
Sick	Work on healing or well-being. Unconscious conflict.	What part of myself am I preparing to heal?
Sidewalk	Life's pathway.	How am I avoiding the mainstream of my life? Where in my life do I want to take my time?
Sideways	Indirect approach.	Where in my life do I wish to be more straightforward?
Silly	Work on dignity or wisdom.	How am I maturing?
Silver	Precious. Flexible. Spiritual strength.	What part of my spirit needs strengthening?
Singing	Joyous celebration. Praise. Communication of feeling.	What do I want to celebrate or communicate?

Image	Associations	Ask Yourself
Sink	Minor release or cleansing.	What incidental issues do I wish to wash away?
Sinking	Descent into unconscious.	How am I ready to get to the bottom of things?
Sister	Feminine self. Fellowship.	What do I admire or judge in myself?
Sitting	Work on relaxation or boredom.	What am I waiting for? Where am I at ease?
Six *See also* **Numbers.**	Expansion. Organization. Harmony. Domesticity.	What am I ready to commit to?
Skateboard	Youthful expression of power. Joyous freedom of movement.	Where in my life do I seek rejuvenation?
Skating *See also* **Ice; Rollerblades.**	Rapid movement with great ease. Grace.	What am I ready to move across with ease?
Skeleton *See also* **Body parts; bone.**	Work on support or structure. Remains.	Where in my life do I feel disconnected or falling apart?
Skiing *See also* **Snow.**	High-speed, active movement. Physical skill and balance.	What part of me is ready to enjoy greater freedom of movement?
Skin *See also* **Body parts.**	Surface of the self. Sensitivity. Connection between inner and outer. Protection.	What is on the surface? What keeps me safe? How am I vulnerable?

Image	Associations	Ask Yourself
Skirt **See also Clothing.**	Lower self. Passions.	What signals am I sending?
Skull	Mortality.	What are my priorities in life? What is important?
Skunk **See also Animals, wild.**	Passive aggression.	Where in my life do I feel the need to protect myself?
Sky	Limitless freedom. Expansion.	Where in my life can I be without limits?
Skydiving **See also Diving; Sky.**	Thrill of loss of control.	What test am I ready to pass?
Skyscraper	Lofty aspiration. Worldly goals.	What do I wish to achieve? How high am I ready to climb?
Slant	Ambivalence. Options.	What do I need to see or understand differently?
Slapping	Force of attention.	What do I wish or fear to draw attention to?
Slaughterhouse	Sacrificial death.	What part of me dies for the rest to survive?
Sledgehammer	Massive destruction.	What am I tearing down?

Image	Associations	Ask Yourself
Sleeping	Unconscious. Deep relaxation and rest.	What part of me is ready to awaken?
Sleeping bag	Shelter. Warmth. Protection.	What part of the unconscious do I wish to safely explore?
Slime/Slimy	Unclean emotions. Revulsion. Untrustworthiness.	What am I ready to clean up?
Slip See also **Clothing.**	Private or inner self.	What do I wish or fear to reveal to the world?
Slow	Patience. Inefficiency.	Where do I take my time? What slows me down?
Slow motion	Repetition. Detail.	What do I want to experience again or more clearly?
Slug See also **Animals, wild.**	Work on laziness. Lack of charm.	Where do I want to take action? What do I judge in myself?
Smart	Work on expertise or intelligence.	What do I wish to know?
Smell	Intuition based on senses.	What do I know if I trust my senses? What smells bad or good in this situation?

Image	Associations	Ask Yourself
Smiling	Work on joy or sorrow.	What makes me happy? What am I longing for?
Smoking/Smoke See also **Cigarette.**	Restricted vision. Residue. Screen.	What is hidden? What do I want to hide?
Smothered	Work on freedom and trust.	Where in my life am I preparing to express my strength?
Smuggling	Work on ownership or control.	What has been denied to me? What do I want to possess?
Snake See also **Animals, wild.**	Energy. The serpent power of kundalini. Sexuality.	What energy am I ready to express or understand?
Sniper	Stealthy attack. Hidden aggression.	What hidden anger am I ready to address?
Snorkeling See also **Swimming.**	Safety with feeling state. Exploration of feelings.	What old emotions do I want to look at?
Snow	Purity. Emotion in suspension. Clarity. Ends and beginnings.	What is over? Where in my life do I want a fresh start?
Soap	Cleansing. Purification.	Do I need to clean up my act?
Socks See also **Clothing.**	Ordinariness. Comfort.	Where in my life do I want more ease?

Image	Associations	Ask Yourself
Soldier	Work on confrontation.	What am I ready to challenge? Where in my life do I fear challenge?
Son	Youthful, masculine aspect of self.	Where in my life am I ready to express youthful power?
Sorrow	Work on grief. Sadness.	What old pain do I wish to heal?
Soul	Essence of being. Spiritual center.	How do I experience my wholeness?
South	Ease. Freedom from constraint. Relaxation.	What part of me seeks release?
South America/South American	Spontaneity. Volatility. Conquest.	What conflict am I ready to master?
Spaceship/Space See also **Outer space; Rocket.**	Exploration of consciousness or inner realms. Transcendence of physical limitations.	What greater consciousness am I seeking or making contact with?
Spam (e-mail)	Cheap communication.	What do I want to avoid or eliminate?
Spam (food)	Cheap satisfaction.	How do I satisfy myself?
Spanking	Work on childish rage.	What part of me wants to grow up?

Image	Associations	Ask Yourself
Speaking	Communication. Message.	What am I telling myself?
Spear See also **Weapon.**	Wounding projectile. Attack from a short distance.	What fears am I ready to look at more closely?
Speeding See also **Vehicles.**	Work on fulfillment.	What will I miss if I don't slow down?
Sperm See also **Sex.**	Fertility. Vitality.	What do I want to create?
Sphinx	Mystery. Riddles.	What secrets do I seek to understand?
Spicy	Flavor. Intensity.	Where in my life do I seek more stimulation? What heightens my experience?
Spider	The dark feminine force. Spinner of webs. Patience. Organization.	Do I fear or admire these qualities in myself?
Spine See also **Body parts.**	Support. Responsibility.	What holds me up?
Spiral	Dynamic movement. Evolution. Cycles.	Where in my life am I growing and expanding?
Spire	Direction of aspirations. Highest goals.	What am I reaching towards? What inspires me?

Image	Associations	Ask Yourself
Spit/Spitting	Insult. Offense.	What annoys me?
Splinter	Minor pain or inconvenience.	What small discomfort am I ready to heal?
Sports	Playing the game. Honor.	What game am I playing?
Spring *See also* Water.	Source. Beginning.	Where in my life am I allowing my feelings new expression?
Spring (season)	Cycle of growth. Generation.	What am I incubating?
Spy	Work on secrecy.	Where in my life am I ready to open up?
Square *See also* Four.	Stability. Matter. Strength. Sudden change.	What in my life is stable for me? Where is my stability about to change?
Squeeze	Concentration.	Where do I need more room?
Squid	Wariness. Strangling.	Where in my life am I ready to be seen or to speak out?
Squirrel *See also* Animals, wild.	Hoarding. Running in place.	Where in my life am I ready to feel more secure?

Image	Associations	Ask Yourself
Stabbing	Fear of betrayal.	Where in my life am I ready to be more trusting?
Stadium	Arena. Exhibition.	What skill am I ready to perform?
Stage	Performance. Achievement.	What recognition do I crave or fear? What am I ready to show to the world?
Stagecoach	Adventurous journey.	In what ways do I seek excitement on my path?
Stairs See also **House.**	Ascent. Going higher. Aspiration. Descent. Grounding.	What do I want to rise or descend to?
Stake	Boundary. Restraint.	What do I wish to separate or tie down?
Stamp	Facility of communication.	What am I ready to say or hear?
Star	Source of light or illumination. Spiritual awakening.	Where in my life am I ready to shine forth?
Statue	Representation. Image.	What content do I wish to give form to?
Steam	Power. Sometimes rage.	What feelings are heating up in me?

Image	Associations	Ask Yourself
Stepfather See also **Father.**	Substitute authority or guidance.	What controls me? What do I care for?
Stepmother See also **Mother.**	Substitute nurturing or tending.	What do I approve of or disapprove of in myself?
Stepping-stones	Safe passage. Secure movement.	What method will get me there?
Stick (object)	Natural tool or weapon. Potential.	What do I wish to make use of?
Stick/Sticking	Clinging.	What won't let go?
Still See also **Calm.**	Calm. Absence of stimulation.	Where do I want more peace in my life?
Stillborn	Failure to trust. Loss of innocence.	Where must I begin again?
Stilts	Balance. View.	What disturbs my equilibrium?
Stock market	Shared wealth or loss.	What risks am I willing to take?
Stomach See also **Body parts.**	Digestion of information or circumstances. Understanding.	What value can I receive from my experience?
Stone See also **Rock.**	Essence. Elemental self. Solidity.	What part of me is solid or impenetrable?

Image	Associations	Ask Yourself
Store	Resources. Variety. Choice.	What new things am I seeking?
Storm	Tumultuous change.	What forces are struggling within me?
Stove	Warmth. Heat. Nourishment. Comfort.	What warms me? What is the source of my security or comfort?
Strange	Originality. Eccentricity.	What makes me different?
Stranger	Unacknowledged aspect of self.	What part of my nature am I ready to know?
Strangling	Holding back communication.	What am I ready to say or hear?
Straw	Common. Fodder.	What is the true value of my simplicity? Where do I seek inner gold?
Stream See also **Water; Creek.**	The flow of feeling.	What feelings flow comfortably within me?
Stress	Work on what can or can't happen.	What feelings do I fear to feel?
Stretch	Flexibility. Extension.	Where do I need to be more adaptable?

Image	Associations	Ask Yourself
String	Joining. Restricting.	What do I wish to tie together? What is confining?
Stripes	Order. Organized effort.	What line am I willing or unwilling to follow?
Stripper/Striptease	Enticement.	What tempts me?
Stroke	Resistance to change. Work on surrender.	What must I change to survive?
Strong	Work on vitality or responsibility.	What am I preparing to take on?
Structure	Beliefs.	What supports me?
Stumble	Minor obstacles. Clumsiness.	How can I move more confidently along my life's path?
Stump	Interrupted or blocked growth.	Have I been growing in the wrong direction? Do I feel thwarted?
Stupid	Work on authority.	What do I respect in myself?
Submarine	Means of exploring unconscious or emotional states.	What feelings am I ready to examine?
Subway	Rapid movement through the unconscious.	What powerful drives can I make conscious use of?

Image	Associations	Ask Yourself
Sudden	Impatience. Excitement. Unexpected.	What am I tired of waiting for?
Suffocation/Suffocating See also **Smothered.**	Restriction. Self-doubt.	What part of me must expand for me to live?
Sugar	Sweetness. Indulgence. Sometimes forbidden pleasure.	What pleasures do I deny myself?
Suicide	Self-destruction. Giving up part of the self.	What part of me must go? What do I want to quit?
Suit See also **Clothing.**	Formality. Professional identity.	What power or ability do I wish to be recognized for?
Summer	Cycle of fruition. Fullness of growth.	What am I producing?
Summit See also **Mountain; Peak; Top.**	Attainment. Goals.	What constitutes success for me?
Sun	Energy. Light. Source. Life-giving power.	What do I wish or fear to receive?
Sundress See also **Clothing.**	Comfortable exposure.	What pleasures am I seeking? What part of me is ready to relax?

Image	Associations	Ask Yourself
Sunglasses *See also* Glasses; Sun.	Disguise. Protection or concealment. Glamour.	How do I wish to be seen? What part of me do I keep from view?
Sunrise	Awakening. Beginning. Hope.	Where in my life am I ready to start over?
Sunset	Rest. Completion of the cycle. Release.	What have I accomplished?
Surfing *See also* Water.	Riding the waves of feeling.	What powerful emotions am I ready to enjoy?
Surgery	Work on healing.	What part of me wants to be well?
Surprise	Wonder. Unexpected.	What changes the way I see or understand things?
Surrender	Work on yielding.	What old patterns or beliefs am I ready to part with?
Survive/Survival	Challenge. Endurance.	What must I do or be to stay alive?
Swamp *See also* Water.	Overwhelming, turgid feelings.	What old emotional patterns are beginning to change for me?
Swan	Grace. Elegance.	How has my beauty been concealed?

Image	Associations	Ask Yourself
Sweating	Intense exertion. Stress.	What requires my effort? What worries me?
Swelling	Out-of-control expansion.	What pressure am I ready to release?
Swimming See also **Water.**	Movement through feeling, often with feelings of accomplishment. Emotion as environment.	What emotional state is deeply satisfying to me? What emotional support do I seek?
Swimming pool See also **Water.**	The water of feeling contained by cultural constructs. Safety.	What feeling do I wish to contain safely?
Swimming underwater	Submersion in emotion.	What feelings am I submerged in?
Sword See also **Weapon.**	Cutting away, especially the past or falsity.	What old ideas or beliefs am I prepared to sever?
Table	Place of activity.	What am I ready to examine or to do?
Talking	Communication.	What am I ready to express? To whom or what do I want to communicate?
Tan See also **Colors.**	Convention. Hard work. Propriety.	In what ways do I seek or avoid respectability?

Image	Associations	Ask Yourself
Tank	Armor. Destructive protection. Mobile threat.	What is dangerous in my expression of power?
Tattoo	Unorthodox self-expression. Display.	What strange message am I ready to convey?
Tavern See also **Bar.**	Conviviality. Relaxation. Indulgence.	What fellowship do I thirst for?
Tea	Contentment. Companionship.	Where in my life am I ready to take my time?
Teacher	Learning. Discipline.	What do I want to know?
Teaching See also **School.**	Work on knowledge or communication.	Where in my life am I ready to acknowledge or share my wisdom?
Tear gas	Torturous feelings. Smothered by suffering.	What deep pain am I ready to wash away?
Tears	Emotional release.	What feelings am I ready to experience?
Teddy bear See also **Toy animal.**	Trust. Protection. Fetish of possession.	What must I trust in order to love and be loved?
Teeth See also **Body parts.**	Independence. Power. Ability to nourish and communicate.	Where in my life do I fear dependence? What do I wish to say?

Image	Associations	Ask Yourself
Telephone	Communication at a distance.	To whom or to what do I want to reach out?
Telescope	Distant vision.	What do I want to observe more closely?
Television	Image or story about reality. Means of observing events.	What story am I creating? What do I want to observe?
Temp See also **Employment; Job.**	Professional transition.	What am I almost ready to do?
Temple See also **Shrine.**	Soul. Sanctuary.	What is the form of my inner peace?
Ten See also **Numbers.**	New beginning on a higher octave. Groups.	What have I learned?
Tent See also **House.**	Temporary house of the self.	What natural part of myself do I wish to reconnect with?
Terror See also **Fear.**	Paralyzing fear. Loss of trust.	What is central to my well-being? What do I trust in myself?
Terrorist	Violence born of frustration.	Where in my life do I feel my power is thwarted?

Image	Associations	Ask Yourself
Test	Ordeal or examination.	What abilities or knowledge am I ready to demonstrate?
Testicles See also **Body parts.**	Yang power. Masculinity.	What power am I ready to express?
Testimony	Story about reality.	What do I believe to be true?
Theater	Performance. Play at being.	What drama do I present?
Theft	Lack. Need. Judgment.	What do I fear I can't have or don't deserve? What am I afraid of losing?
Therapist	Work on self-acceptance and love.	What parts of myself are ready for integration?
Thigh See also **Body parts.**	Power of movement.	Am I strong enough to get where I want to go?
Thin	Asceticism. Elegance. Self-denial.	What am I hungry for?
Third World	Absence of development.	What do I need to advance?
Thirty-three See also **Numbers.**	Salvation and temptation.	Where in my life have I succeeded or failed?

Image	Associations	Ask Yourself
Thorn *See also* Splinter.	Prick of awareness.	What awakens me?
Thread	Frailty. Fragility.	What am I ready to strengthen?
Three *See also* Numbers; Triangle.	Trinity. Balance of opposites. Sociability.	How do I integrate my differences?
Throat *See also* Body parts.	Communication. Trust. Creativity.	What am I ready to hear and say?
Thugs	Ugly forms of power. Misuse of energy.	Where in my life am I ready to clean up my act? How is power threatening to me?
Tick	Energy sucking.	What exhausts me?
Ticket	Means of admission.	What new experience or destination am I heading for?
Tidal wave *See also* Water.	Overwhelming emotion.	What feelings are threatening to me?
Tiger *See also* Animals, wild.	Power. Wild beauty. Sexual force.	What is dangerous in me?
Tightrope	No options. Balance.	How am I ready to make my life easier?

Image	Associations	Ask Yourself
Tights See also **Clothing.**	Shaping. Firming.	What can I safely expose?
Time	Attachment. Organization.	Where in my life am I ready to be carefree?
Tired	Stress. Hopelessness.	What respite do I seek?
Tires See also **Vehicles.**	Cushion. Shock absorption.	Where in my life do I need to smooth my way?
Toad See also **Animals, wild.**	Infectious ugliness.	How or why have I concealed my true beauty?
Toe See also **Body parts.**	Beginning, especially of movement.	Where am I preparing to go?
Tombstone	Memorial. Record.	How do I wish to be remembered? What do I leave behind?
Tongue See also **Body parts.**	The pleasure of taste.	What am I eager to try?
Tonsils See also **Body parts: throat.**	Stifled expression of emotion or of creativity.	What am I preparing to share?
Tools	Work on productivity.	What do I want to do or create?

Image	Associations	Ask Yourself
Top See also **Above**.	Higher understanding or knowledge. Culmination. Resolution. Perfection.	To what do I aspire? What point have I reached?
Topless See also **Breast**.	Exposure. Invitation.	How do I exhibit love?
Tornado	Violent force of destruction.	What dramatic change can I see approaching?
Torture	Part of the self tormented by the rest.	How am I hard on myself?
Touch/Touching	Direct contact.	What or whom do I want to reach?
Tourniquet See also **Blood**.	Work on loss of strength.	Where am I feeling drained?
Tower	Rise above. Ascendancy. Sometimes isolation.	What accomplishment do I seek or fear?
Toy animal See also **Animals, domestic; Animals, wild.**	Playful relationship with the natural world. Freedom from responsibility.	Where do I want more pleasure in my life?
Toys	Youthful play. Practicing life's responsibilities.	In what way am I ready to enjoy my life more?
Tractor	Sturdiness. Resourcefulness.	What am I processing?

Image	Associations	Ask Yourself
Traffic See also **Vehicles.**	Chaotic power or movement.	What prevents me from going where I want or need to go?
Traffic jam See also **Vehicles.**	Frustrated power or movement.	Where is my energy blocked?
Trail See also **Path.**	Life's path.	How safe is my chosen route?
Trailer See also **Vehicles.**	Following. Impediment.	What extra load do I carry?
Trailer house	Mobile self-image. Sometimes self-scorn.	What do I judge or accept about myself and my predecessors?
Trailer park	Squalor.	How do I hope to trade up? Where do I feel diminished?
Train See also **Travel;** **Vehicles.**	Movement made while observing the areas covered or traveled.	What do I wish to observe as I change my life?
Trance See also **Channeling.**	Altered state. Expanded consciousness.	What part of my inner self am I ready to explore?
Transit	Change.	What am I leaving behind or heading towards?

Image	Associations	Ask Yourself
Transmission See also **Vehicles**.	Adjustment to circumstance.	Where am I speeding up or slowing down?
Transplant	New life.	What part of me feels worn out? Where in my life do I seek renewal?
Trap	Work on freedom or liberty.	What am I extricating myself from?
Travel/Traveling See also **Vehicles**.	Movement from one way of life or attitude to another. Life's journey.	Where am I going? Where do I want to go?
Treasure	Fulfillment. Integration. Material or spiritual reward.	What do I need to feel complete?
Tree See also **Wood**.	Natural process. Structure of life.	Where in my life am I ready to grow?
Trench	Hiding place. Concealment.	Where in my life do I need to feel safe? What do I want to hide?
Trial	Test. Resolution of conflict.	What is at issue?
Triangle See also **Three**.	Dynamic power. Integration of opposites.	Where in my life am I developing power by integrating internal opposition?

Image	Associations	Ask Yourself
Trick or treat	Lottery of life.	What am I hoping to receive? What do I resent?
Tricycle See also **Vehicles.**	Immature power. Playful movement.	Am I mature enough to get there? An I enjoying the journey?
Tropics	Torrid. Luxuriant.	What do I wish to indulge myself in?
Trousers See also **Clothing.**	Lower self. Passions.	What signals am I sending?
Trout See also **Fish.**	Elusivity. Nimbleness.	Where am I preparing to adapt my feelings?
Truck See also **Vehicles.**	Ability to carry the load.	Can I handle the responsibility?
Trunk (tree)	Sturdiness or weakness.	What supports me?
Trust fund	Security. Control.	How am I ready to take care of myself?
Trusting	Work on self-acceptance.	What part of myself am I ready to integrate?
Truth	Security of belief.	What supports me?
T-shirt See also **Clothing: shirt.**	Relaxed self-image. Youth.	Where do I want to take it easy?

Image	Associations	Ask Yourself
Tumor	Protective growth.	What old pain am I ready to release?
Tunnel	Path through inner space. Ordeal.	What light leads me on?
Turban See also **Clothing**.	Mystery. Glamour. Whimsy.	How am I confined by convention?
Turquoise See also **Colors**.	Healing. Good luck. Protection.	Where in my life do I feel safe?
Turtle See also **Animals, wild**.	Protection. Perseverance.	Where in my life do I feel safe when I take my time?
Twenty-two See also **Numbers**.	Earthly mission. Self and others.	What do I trust?
Twigs	Small growth.	Where in my life am I growing?
Twin	Work on identity. Mirror image.	What do I reflect?
Two See also **Numbers**.	Duality. Opposition. Balance. Partnership. Equality.	How do I relate?
Tyrant	Work on freedom.	What limits or confines me?

Image	Associations	Ask Yourself
UFO *See also* **Alien.**	Fear and joy of the unknown. Distant realms.	Where am I ready to expand into unknown realms?
Ugly	Work on rejection or judgment.	What repels me? How am I improving myself?
Umbilical cord	Link between old and new self.	How am I connected with my emerging self?
Umbrella	Protection from emotional storms.	What is raining down on me?
Umpire *See also* **Judge.**	Work on fair play.	Where do I seek impartiality?
Under *See also* **Bottom.**	Unconscious. Lower aspect of self.	What am I ready to bring forth?
Underground	Unconscious material.	What is ready to rise to consciousness?
Underwater *See also* **Swimming; Water.**	Submersion in emotion.	What emotions am I submerged within?
Underwear *See also* **Clothing.**	Private self. Sexual identity.	What are my hidden feelings?
Undressing	Exposing true or inner self.	Who am I underneath it all?

Image	Associations	Ask Yourself
Unfeeling	Work on denial of emotion.	Where in my life am I prepared to be less sensitive?
Unicorn	Purity. Magical consciousness. Union of the divine and animal nature.	Where in my life am I ready to align my animal nature with my spiritual essence?
Uniform See also **Clothing**.	Conformity.	Where in my life do I wish to share with others or to break free of rules?
Universe	Totality of being. Wholeness.	Where in my life do I feel complete?
University See also **School**.	Higher learning.	What knowledge do I wish to expand?
Up	Conscious self. Higher consciousness.	What do I aspire to?
Upside down	Reversal. Confusion.	What do I want to straighten out?
Urine/Urinating See also **Bathroom**.	Release, usually of emotion. Anger. Embarrassment at emotional release.	What feelings am I clearing? Am I pissed off?
Vaccination	Protective injection.	What am I afraid of catching?

Image	Associations	Ask Yourself
Vacuum	Emptiness. Absence. Potential.	What is missing? What fills me?
Vacuum cleaner	Cleanliness. Order.	What do I want to be rid of? What am I cleaning up?
Vagina See also **Body parts.**	Female sexuality. Yin receptivity.	What do I receive? What receives me?
Valley	Protection. Safety. Ease.	What makes me comfortable?
Vamp	Work on ability to attract.	What do I need to feel desirable? What tempts me?
Vampire	Energy-draining fear.	What pursues me? Where in my life do I deny my own power?
Van See also **Vehicles.**	Practical power. Convenience.	How do I share my power? How much or how many can I carry?
Vase	Receptivity. Display.	What am I ready to receive?
Vegetable	Healthy food. Natural sustenance.	What am I hungry for?
Vehicles See also *subheadings.*	Power. Movement. What gets you there.	How powerful am I? How do I feel about power?

Image	Associations	Ask Yourself
— *bicycle*	Self-propulsion. Recreation.	Do I have enough strength to make it? Will it be fun?
— *boat*	Movement across the depths of feeling.	What emotions can I safely negotiate?
— *brakes*	Control or slowing of movement.	Where in my life am I ready to feel more secure with my power?
— *bus*	Shared journey. Mass transit.	How does my personal power relate to mass consciousness?
— *car*	Personal power. Ego.	Can I get there? Who am I?
— *convertible*	Glamorous power. Parade.	What power am I ready to display?
— *helicopter*	Movement in many directions.	Where in my life do I want more freedom of movement?
— *hydrofoil*	Soaring above the sea of feeling.	What emotions no longer inhibit me?
— *jeep*	Ruggedness. Utility. Efficiency.	Where in my life must I be sturdy to reach my goal?

Image	Associations	Ask Yourself
— *limousine*	Luxurious power. Extravagance.	Where in my life am I ready to be conspicuous in my expression of power?
— *motorcycle*	Virility. Vigor. Display.	How hot am I? Where in my life am I ready to be more masterful?
— *plane*	Rapid movement across great distance.	Am I in a hurry for change?
— *R.V.*	The joy of power. Rugged amusement.	Where in my life am I ready to have more fun with my power?
— *seat belt*	Safety restraint.	What holds my power in check?
— *speeding*	Work on fulfillment.	What will I miss if I don't slow down?
— *tires*	Cushion. Shock absorption.	Where in my life do I need to smooth the way?
— *traffic*	Chaotic power or movement.	What prevents me from going where I want or need to go?
— *traffic jam*	Frustrated power or movement.	Where is my energy blocked?
— *trailer*	Following. Impediment.	What extra load do I carry?

Image	Associations	Ask Yourself
— *train*	Movement made while observing the areas covered or traveled.	What do I wish to observe as I change my life?
— *tricycle*	Immature power. Playful movement.	Am I mature enough to get there? Am I enjoying the journey?
— *truck*	Ability to carry the load.	Can I take on the responsibility?
— *van*	Practical power. Convenience.	How do I share my power? How much or how many can I carry?
Veil *See also* Clothing.	Illusion. Mystery.	What do I want to hide or to reveal?
Velvet	Softness. Luxury.	What is too hard for me? Where in my life am I vulnerable?
Verdict	Judgment.	What do I fear or hope is true?
Veteran	Survivor of conflict.	What battle is over for me?
Video games	High-tech competition. Skill. Dexterity.	What new abilities are available to me?
View	Expanded vision.	What enlarges my world?

Image	Associations	Ask Yourself
Village	Community. Simplicity. Rusticity.	What traditional beliefs do I honor or reject?
Violet See also **Colors.**	Spirituality. Boundary between visible and invisible realms. Aristocracy.	To what do I aspire?
Vise	Squeeze. Connection.	Where do I feel confined or connected?
Visible	New information.	What am I ready to see or to know?
Vitamins	Vitality. Support.	Where do I want more vigor in my life?
Voice	Personal power. Identity.	What do I want to say or hear?
Voiceless	Retreat. Loss of identity.	What will happen if I make myself heard?
Volcano	Eruption of unconscious or repressed material.	What must I clear?
Volunteer	Work on willingness.	What do I have to offer? What do I stand up for?
Vomit/Vomiting	Throwing up indigestible thoughts or feelings.	What do I need to get rid of?

Image	Associations	Ask Yourself
Vote/Voting	Choice.	Who or what do I identify with?
Voyeurism See also **Sex.**	Safe distance from desires.	What do I want or fear to be close to?
Vulture	Scavenger.	How am I nourished by the experience of my past?
Waiter/Waitress	Work on service. Servility.	What service am I ready to provide? Where am I tired of serving?
Waiting	Boredom. Frustration.	Where am I ready to act or to move?
Walk/Walking	Natural movement. Exercise. Progress.	Where am I going? Am I moving fast enough?
Wall See also **House.**	Barrier. Defense. Partition. Protection.	What am I ready to integrate? What separation is necessary for me? What is on the other side?
Walrus See also **Animals, wild.**	Massive sensitivity.	Where in my life am I ready to be less threatening?
War	Conflict. Violent resolution.	What parts of me are in conflict? What must be decided despite the cost?

Image	Associations	Ask Yourself
Warehouse	Storage of resources.	What am I ready to put away or to unpack?
Warrior See also **Soldier; Veteran; War.**	Work on challenges.	What am I ready to dare or to confront?
Wart	Noxious growth. Ugliness.	Where in my life am I ready to be more attractive?
Wasp	Stinging anger.	Where in my life do I want to strike out?
Wasting	Despair. Exhaustion.	How is my energy being depleted?
Watch See also **Clock; Time.**	Limitation. Division.	Where in my life do I want to be carefree?
Watching	Neutrality. Aloofness.	What do I hesitate to join, or wish to join?
Water See also **subheadings; Elements.**	Emotion. Dissolving. Yielding. Fluid. Release. Cleansing.	What am I feeling?
— bay	Shelter. Enclosure.	Where do I feel calm?
— creek	The flow of feeling.	What feelings flow comfortably within me?
— dew	Gentle release of emotion.	What feelings can I safely express?

Image	Associations	Ask Yourself
— *dripping*	Trickle of emotion.	What am I releasing, bit by bit?
— *faucet*	Control or release of emotion.	What feelings do I turn on and off?
— *flood*	Overflow of emotion.	What feelings are too much for me?
— *fountain*	Emotion springing forth. Freedom of emotional expression. Release.	What feelings are welling up in me?
— *frozen*	Preservation. Restraint.	What rigid feelings am I ready to dissolve?
— *harbor*	Shelter. Safety.	Where in my life do I find emotional peace?
— *hose*	Flexibility. Flow of emotion.	How well do I communicate my feelings?
— *ice*	A rigid feeling state. Frozen.	What feelings are locked within or ready to be melted away?
— *lake*	Contained emotion. Often a sense of tranquility or peace.	What feelings do I comfortably contain?
— *melting*	Letting go.	What old structures am I ready to dissolve?

Image	Associations	Ask Yourself
— *mist*	Delicate expanse of feeling. Cool and comfortable.	What emotional field surrounds me?
— *mud*	Messy feelings. Fertility. Stuck.	What emotions am I ready to clean up?
— *ocean*	Vast, limitless feeling. Sometimes an overwhelming emotion. Rich with abundant life.	What part of me relates to such vastness?
— *pond*	Contained feelings. Tranquility.	What emotions do I hold close?
— *puddle*	Small but messy emotions.	What minor discomfort am I feeling?
— *rain*	Release of emotion. May be gentle and nourishing or dramatically threatening.	What feelings are pouring down on me?
— *rapids*	Active, stimulating emotions.	How comfortable am I with intense feelings?
— *reef*	Danger or safety of hidden emotions.	What underlies my feelings?
— *river*	Flowing and active. May include dangerous rapids; may be smooth and tranquil.	What feelings are actively moving within me?

Image	Associations	Ask Yourself
— *spring*	Source. Beginning.	Where in my life am I allowing my feelings new expression?
— *swamp*	Overwhelming, turgid feelings.	What old emotional patterns are beginning to change for me?
— *swimming pool*	The water of feeling contained by cultural constructs. Safety.	What feeling do I wish to safely contain?
— *tidal wave*	Overwhelming emotion.	What feelings are threatening to me?
— *waterfall*	Dramatic going with the flow. May be frightening or powerfully releasing.	Where in my life am I ready to take the plunge?
— *waterfront*	Dangerous or untrustworthy feelings.	What emotions are threatening to me?
— *wave*	Activated emotion.	What feelings are coming up in me?
— *well*	Source. Shared resources.	What feelings am I ready to share?
— *wet*	Soaked with feeling.	What emotions cause me discomfort or inconvenience?

Image	Associations	Ask Yourself
— *wet suit*	Safety and comfort in the realm of feeling.	What depths of emotion do I want to safely explore?
Waterfront See also **Water.**	Dangerous or untrustworthy feelings.	What emotions are threatening to me?
Wave See also **Water.**	Activated emotion.	What feelings are coming up in me?
Weak	Inadequacy. Work on force.	Where am I ready to build strength?
Weapon	Work on expression of energy. Offense and defense. Aggression.	Where in my life am I ready to be more open and receptive?
Weasel	Shifty. Deceitful.	Where does my trust fail?
Weaving	Fabrication. Intimacy.	What am I putting together?
Web See also **Spider.**	Communication. Network. Skill. Trap.	What do I wish to control or to understand? What holds me back?
Wedding See also **Marriage.**	Celebration of union.	What do I joyously unite with?
Weed	Rugged fertility. Undesired growth.	What am I cultivating?

Image	Associations	Ask Yourself
Weight	Work on strength. Burdens.	What keeps me in shape or encumbers me?
Weight lifting *See also* **Exercise; Weight.**	Strength developed through effort. Making light of burdens.	How do my responsibilities make me strong?
Well *See also* **Water.**	Source. Shared resources.	What feelings am I ready to share?
Werewolf	Monstrous instincts.	What part of me is overcivilized? Where in my life are my instincts repressed?
West	Ending. Death. Return to beginning.	Where am I heading?
Wet *See also* **Water.**	Soaked with feeling.	What emotions cause me discomfort or inconvenience?
Wet suit *See also* **Water.**	Safety and comfort in the realm of feeling.	What depths of emotion do I want to safely explore?
Whale *See also* **Animals, wild.**	Power of the unconscious. Truth and strength of inner being.	What great truth am I ready to accept?
Wheel	Repetition. Totality.	What moves me to completion?
Wheelchair *See also* **Vehicles.**	Work on mobility, despite limitation.	Where do I feel loss of power?

Image	Associations	Ask Yourself
Whip/Whipping See also **Sex:** **sadomasochism.**	Punishment. Dangerous excitement.	Where or what do I wish to control?
White See also **Colors.**	Purity. Clarity. Coldness.	What do I seek to purify?
Wide	Greater understanding or access.	Where do I need more room?
Widow/Widower	Solitude. Isolation.	What part of me is lonely?
Wife	Yin aspect of self. Partner.	What have I joined with?
Wild	Freedom from inhibition. Untamed.	How do beliefs restrict me?
Wind/Windy	Stimulation. Sensory overload.	Where in my life do I seek stimulation? Where do I feel overwhelmed?
Windmill See also **Wind.**	Power of movement. Stimulating force.	What powerful thoughts are stirring within me?
Window See also **House.**	Vision. Seeing and being seen.	What am I willing to see? What do I wish to reveal or conceal?
Wine See also **Alcohol;** **Drunk.**	Conviviality. Celebration.	What do I wish to enjoy?

Image	Associations	Ask Yourself
Wing	Flight. Freedom. Transcendence.	What am I ready to rise above?
Winning	Success. Victory.	What old self-doubts am I defeating?
Winter	Cycle of disintegration. Rest. Rebirth.	What am I preparing to bring forth?
Wise	Independence of mind and spirit.	What factions no longer interest me?
Wish	Hope. Belief in the future.	What do I long for?
Witch	Negative feminine. Black magic. If positive, intuition and natural wisdom.	What feminine power do I hold or fear?
Witchcraft	Manipulation of reality, or fear of manipulation of reality.	Who or what controls my world?
Witness/Witnessing	Detachment.	Where do I hold back from participation in events?
Wizard	Work on skill or sorcery.	What powers do I seek to master?
Wolf See also **Animals, wild.**	Instinct. Appetite. Threat. Loyalty.	What instincts are a threat to me? What are my instinctive loyalties?

Image	Associations	Ask Yourself
Woman	Feminine aspect. Receptivity.	Where in my life am I ready to be more receptive?
Wood See also **Lumber; Tree.**	Growth.	What is my natural form?
Wool	Coziness. Natural protection.	What keeps me warm?
Workshop	Process. Self-understanding.	What skills do I wish to develop?
Worm	Decay. Insignificance.	Where in my life am I ready to assert myself?
Wound/Wounded	Site of grief or anguish.	What damage am I ready to heal?
Wreck	Violent destruction. Barrier to progress. Rejection.	What or who wants to stop me? What am I ready to restore?
Wrestling	Work on strength and stamina.	What am I struggling to understand or control?
Wrinkle	Old or new ideas.	What have I learned?
Writing	Self-expression. Record of experience.	What do I wish to put on record?
X ray	Seeing inside. Dangerous energies.	What lies within? What do I fear if I penetrate the surface image?

Image	Associations	Ask Yourself
Yard *See also* **Garden; Grass.**	Enclosure. Personal space.	What surrounds me?
Yarn	Binding. Patterns.	What am I connecting or creating?
Yawning	Boredom. Lack of energy.	What will stimulate me?
Yelling	Emotional release.	What must I forcefully express?
Yellow *See also* **Colors.**	Vitality. Intellect. Clarity.	What do I wish to understand?
Yeti *See also* **Animals, wild.**	Man-beast. Legendary.	What part of my greater self is stalking me?
Young/Youth	Immaturity. Vitality.	What part of me is blossoming?
Zero	Beginning or end.	What arises? What is over?
Zigzag	Indecision. Adaptability.	How must my direction change?
Zodiac	Archetypes. Aspects of consciousness.	How do I relate to my own divine nature?
Zombie	Living death.	What am I afraid to let go of?
Zoo *See also* **Animals, wild.**	Wildness under control.	What instincts do I want to observe or enjoy in safety?

Resources for
☾ # Rewarding
Dream Work

Dream incubation tapes offer you an efficient, convenient means of intensifying and directing your dreams. Each tape begins with a guided meditation that relaxes your body and clears your mind, producing a relaxed-body, alert-mind state. The tapes then guide you to create intense images and visions that will lead to stimulating and memorable dreams. The original music that accompanies the tapes was produced for the series by the internationally acclaimed composer Deuter.

Series I/Tape 1

Dream Clearing will unblock old images and recurrent dream patterns that may have been limiting your dream memory for years. (7:33 min.)

Dream Recall stimulates each sense with vivid images. The result is intense dream imagery and better recall of dreams. (8:39 mins.)

Series I/Tape 2

Dream Guidance leads to a dream meeting with the aspect of yourself that can guide you comfortably and securely into knowledge of your own future. (8:41 mins.)

Dream Healing offers guided imagery leading you to Epidauros — healing center of the ancient world — to receive dreams that stimulate healing on an inner level. (8:41 mins.)

Series I/Tape 3

Dream Exploration takes you into dream adventures where you explore other realms of consciousness while your body safely and comfortably sleeps. (10:55 mins.)

The Black Velvet Room opens a dream world of sensuous pleasure and deep, refreshing sleep — an antidote to even the most stressful waking life. It can also be used as a remedy for insomnia. (9:56 mins.)

Series II/Tape 1

Dreamsex helps you explore the depths of your own sexuality in the privacy and safety of the dream state. Opening the dream door to sexual fulfillment often leads to greater creative vitality in your waking life. (18:37 mins.)

The Corridor of Dreams encourages dreams offering specific information about your future projects — including their most likely outcome and barriers to their success. (20:22 mins.)

Series II/Tape 2

Dreamlover leads to a meeting in the dream state with your ideal other, to an aspect of self that is ready for integration, or to actual future lovers. (18:38 mins.)

The Dark Vessel uses the classic imagery of setting out in a small boat across an expanse of dark water — leading the dreamer to contact friends and relatives who are dead. It is also valuable for the terminally ill and those who wish to explore the after-death state. (20:13 mins.)

Order Form

Beyond Your Wildest Dreams: Dream Incubation Tapes, Series I and II

All prices include postage and handling. For delivery outside the U.S., please add an additional $2 per order.

Please send me:

Series No.	Item Description	Price each	Total cost
Series I	All three tapes of Series I	$28.50	_____
Series I	Dream Clearing/Dream Recall	$12.00	_____
Series I	Dream Guidance/Dream Healing	$12.00	_____
Series I	Dream Exploration/Black Velvet Room	$12.00	_____
Series II	Both tapes of Series II	$22.50	_____
Series II	Dreamsex/Corridor of Dreams	$12.00	_____
Series II	Dreamlover/Dark Vessel	$12.00	_____
		Total	$_____

Make check or money order payable to:

Real Dreams, 53-086 Halai Road, Hau`ula HI 96717

Method of payment: Check ____ Money order ____ Visa ____ Mastercard ____

Credit Card Account Number: _____

Expiration: ____ / ____

Credit card orders must include a signature.

Signature:_____Date:____

(please print)

Name: _____

Address: _____

City: _____ State: _____ Zip: _____

Mail to: Real Dreams 53-086 Halai Rd., Hau`ula, HI 96717, or fax to 808-293-8233

Invitation to Readers

Below is a space for you to jot down images you have not found listed in the Basic Dream Images and would like to see included in a future edition of *Understand Your Dreams*. We will be delighted to receive your comments and recommendations. Please fax to 808-293-8233, e-mail to Alice Anne at Parkerdreams@aol.com, or mail to Real Dreams, 53-086 Halai Rd. Hau`ula, HI 96717.

(Index

☾ About the Author

A sought after professional psychic and recognized dream counselor, Alice Anne Parker has taught dream workshops and healing intensives around the world since 1973. She has appeared frequently as a dream expert on the internationally broadcast Gary Null show, and has been a guest on the national CNBC television show, "Alive and Wellness." In Honolulu, Alice Anne produced and hosted Dreamline, a live, call-in radio show on dreams and has written a regular feature on dreams for Body Mind Spirit magazine.

Her book, *Understand Your Dreams: 1500 Basic Dream Images and How to Interpret Them,* first published in 1991 and reissued in an expanded edition in 1995, has sold more than 60,000 copies worldwide. She is also the author of the metaphysical adventure novel, *The Last of the Dream People.*

Parker is a Phi Beta Kappa graduate of Hunter College in New York City and holds a master's degree from Columbia University. She cultivated her psychic abilities with the renowned teacher Dr. Thomas Maughan, Chief of the Ancient Order of Druids, in Great Britain. She is an award-winning filmmaker, whose seven short films have been honored at the Cannes Film Festival, the New York Film Festival, the Venice Bienalle, and a one-person show at the Whitney Museum of American Art. Parker shares her dreams and her life with her husband, Henry Holthaus, in Hau`ula, Hawaii.

Please visit her website, AliceAnneParker.com for information on upcoming workshops and to preview soon-to-be-published books, or contact her directly at Parkerdreams@aol.com.

Mysterious. Erotic. Hauntingly Beautiful.

Learn how you can use the dream teachings of the fabulous and mysterious S'norra people to unveil the deeper meaning of your own dreams, and empower you to act on their guidance.

Praise for *The Last of the Dream People*

"A compelling tale told by a master storyteller of a mysterious and innocent native people whose dreams are instruments of guidance and prophecy. *The Last of the Dream People* will help unveil the deeper meaning of your own dreams and empower you to act upon their guidance."

— LaUna Huffines, author of *Healing Yourself with Light*

"I read your book as soon as I got it and greatly enjoyed it.... The way I test a new book is to read the first paragraph. So I read yours. The next thing I knew I'd read the whole book. Thanks again. I'll see you in my dreams."

— Bill Martin, artist

"In this wonderful book, Alice Anne Parker establishes herself as a magnificent storyteller and spiritual teacher. I was unable to put it down."

— Michael Peter Langevin, copublisher of *Magical Blend Magazine*

"A hauntingly beautiful tale. . . . Parker has taken her ability for dream analysis to a new level."
— Carol Adrienne, coauthor of *The Celestine Prophecy*

"My senses were awakened by the eroticism of the love story and the gripping tale of adventure. Only on reflection did I appreciate that you were using your mighty spiritual power to teach me how to connect with the deeper significance of my own dreams."
— Sheila Rainer, bestselling author of *The Language of Flowers*

"Skillfully blends the conscious with the superconscious, the act with the consequence, and the illusion of reality with the reality of the intuitive."
— Elizabeth Engstrom, author of *Lizard Wine*

"I just read — almost in one sitting — *The Last of the Dream People*. Your book had me spellbound."
— Robert Wolff, author of *What It Is to Be Human* and *The Spiral*

"Alice Anne reveals a rich terrain; one we visit yet are rarely aware of. . . . Revelatory."
— Terence Stamp, actor

"Vivid and captivating, this is a novel that immerses us in another world, while opening up provocative possibilities for our own."
— Rosie Parker, therapist

"Just finished *Dream People*, which I did enjoy. It was like going to the cinema. I had vivid dreams while reading the book — it was great!"
— Nic Barlow, photographer